Six Weeks in the Sioux Tepees

Six Weeks in the Sioux Tepees

SARAH F. WAKEFIELD

TWODOT®

GUILFORD, CONNECTICUT
HELENA, MONTANA
AN IMPRINT OF THE GLOBE PEQUOT PRESS

A · TWODOT® · BOOK

Text design: Lisa Reneson

Library of Congress Cataloging-in-Publication Data
Wakefield, Sarah F.
 Six weeks in the Sioux tepees / Sarah F. Wakefield. — 1st ed.
  p. cm.
 "A TwoDot book"—T.p. verso
 Originally published: Minneapolis : Atlas Print. Co., 1863.
 ISBN 0-7627-3080-3
  1. Wakefield, Sarah F. 2. Dakota Indians—History. 3. Dakota Indians—Wars, 1862–1865. 4. Indian captivities—Minnesota. 5. Minnesota—Biography. I. Title.

E83.86.W35W35 2004
977.6004'975243—dc22   2003062500

Manufactured in the United States of America
First Edition/First Printing

Editor's Note

*F*irst written in 1863, recounting a harrowing six weeks of captivity with the Sioux Indians in Minnesota, Sarah F. Wakefield's story is a classic narrative of survival. Kidnapped with her two small children in the midst of a struggle between the Sioux and Chippewa that was compounded by the ineffectiveness of the U.S. government Indian Agents dispatched to the region, the privileged doctor's wife suffered from privation and terror. Believing her husband dead and continually in fear for the lives of herself and her children, she used all of her wits to survive, assisted by some of her captors as she hoped for a rescue by the U.S. Army.

Upon her rescue, she penned her tale in response to the difficulties she faced when she was restored to her own home and ostracized for her sympathetic views of her protectors among the Sioux and her respect for their culture. However, she was a product of her upbringing and environment, and her writings about her experience reflect the biases and stereotypes of the time period in spite of her relatively enlightened views. *Six Weeks in the Sioux Tepees* is a fascinating look at one woman's experience of the lifestyle of the Sioux Indians and a testament to her will to survive.

Helena, Mont., 2004

Preface

I wish to say a few words in preface to my Narrative:—First, that when I wrote it, it was not intended for perusal by the public eye. I wrote it for the especial benefit of my children, as they were so young at the time they were in captivity, that in case of my death, they would, by recourse to this, be enabled to recall to memory the particulars; and I trust all who may read it will bear in mind that I do not pretend to be a book-writer, and will not expect to find much to please the mind's fancy. Secondly, I have written a *true* statement of my captivity: what I suffered, and what I was spared from suffering, by a few Friendly or Christian Indians (whether from policy or other motives, time will determine.) Thirdly, I do not publish a little work like this in the expectation of making money from it, but to vindicate myself, as I have been grievously abused by many, who are ignorant of the particulars of my captivity and release by the Indians. I trust all errors will be overlooked, and that the world will not censure me for speaking kindly of those who saved me from death and dishonor, while my own people were so long—Oh! so long!—to come to my rescue.

In placing this pamphlet before the public, I have been subjected to many embarrassments, among the most unpleasant of which is, through malice and gross carelessness of the printer, a number of omissions and misprints have occurred, some of the latter of which I wish to correct. Where the name of "Wara-coto-mong," occurs, it should be spelled *Maza coota mony;* "Mare-Shoe" should be *Muza Shaw;* "Pajuta Wacusta-Tanica" should be *Pajuta Wicaste Tawica;* and instead of "Hardwood," *Hazelwood* should occur.

Sarah F. Wakefield
Shakopee, Minn., Nov. 25th, 1863

*I*n June, 1861, my husband was appointed physician for the upper Sioux Indians, at Pajutazee, or Yellow Medicine.

The first year of our stay it was very quiet, the Indians soon after they were paid leaving for their homes far away, with the exception of those who were farmers, and were living near us as neighbors. And I will state in the beginning that I found them very kind, good people. The women sewed for me, and I have employed them in various ways around my house, and began to love and respect them as well as if they were whites. I became so much accustomed to them and their ways, that when I was thrown into their hands as a prisoner, I felt more easy and contented than any other white person among them, for I knew that not one of the Yellow Medicine Indians would see me and my children suffer as long as they could protect us.

In the spring of 1862, the Agent, accompanied by my husband and others, visited the Indians living near Big Stone Lake, *Lac Frara*, and that vicinity. They found the Indians quiet, and well contented in what was being done for them, and they seemed much pleased with their visitors.

Before leaving, Maj. Galbraith said to them not to come down until he sent for them, as he had doubts respecting the time of payment. He had not been home many weeks when they began coming in, a few at first frightened by some murders committed among them by Chippewas. Not long was it before the whole tribe arrived and camped about one mile from the Agency buildings.

Here they remained many weeks, suffering hunger: every day expecting their pay so as to return to their homes.

After repeatedly asking for food, and receiving none of consequence, they were told by the interpreter, who belonged to Fort Ridgley, and who accompanied the soldiers to Yellow Medicine a few weeks before the arrival of the Indians, to break into the ware house and help themselves, promising them that he would prevent the soldiers from firing upon them.

I think it was the fourth day of August, that the Indians commenced hostilities at Yellow Medicine. We were much surprised early Monday morning, hearing them singing and shouting so early in the day. Soon they came driving down the hill towards the Agency, dressed very finely, and as we thought, for a dance; but we were soon convinced they meant mischief, as they surrounded the soldiers' camp, while part of them rushed up to the ware house and began cutting and beating the door to pieces, all the while shouting, singing and throwing their blankets around them like wild men as they were—driven wild by hunger.

I was with my children up stairs in my own house. My husband's office being in the building connected with the ware house. I was very much frightened, and called my girl to fasten the gate and come in and secure the lower part of the house. Soon they commenced filling our gardens, and all adjoining. In a short time they surrounded our house, and some came to the door and rapped violently. I caught up a pistol and went down the stairs, opened the door, and inquired as calmly as I could what they wanted. They wished axes, and filled the room and followed me around until I gave them all we had. I expected they would kill me, but I knew I could raise an alarm with my pistol before they could get my children. But they offered no violence, and departed quietly; all they cared for was food—it was not our lives; and if all these Indians had been properly fed and otherwise treated like human beings, how many, very many innocent lives might have been spared.

In ten minutes time, after surrounding the ware house, the door opened and they were carrying out flour. Soon, however, the soldiers came to the building and they were obliged to evacuate the premises, but not without many ugly threats and savage looks. The Agent went out and counciled with them, and asked them to give up their flour; but they refused, and he was compelled to give them all they had taken and much more before they would leave. That night there was little sleep at the Agency; all were expecting an attack before morning.

Just at sunrise next morning, a friendly or Christian Indian came and told us the Indians were preparing to make an attack; as they had succeeded so well the day before they would try again. We all knew that matters would be different a second time, as the soldiers intended on firing upon them if they came.

Several families concluded to go down to the Lower Agency, which was thirty miles below us—myself and children being among the number. We remained a week, and while I was there I attended Mr. Hindman's church, and was much pleased with the behavior of the Indians during service. Little did I think while I sat there that my life and my children's would so soon be in danger, and that our deliverer would be one of those wild men that were listening with eager attention to God's word. Surely the missionaries have done good; for where would the white captives now be if the Christian Indians had not taken an interest in their welfare? Monday, August 11th, I returned to my home, my husband coming for me, and saying that the upper Indians had left very quietly, Major Galbraith giving them goods and provisions, and promising to send for them as soon as their money came. I went home with the determination of preparing my clothing for a journey East in a few days, as we were fearful some of the Indians might return and would be troublesome, stealing and begging all summer.

Many who read these pages may not understand about the Indian payment. I will say a few words respecting it: In June these people usually come in for their pay for the lands which they had sold to the United States, some coming many hundreds of miles; and if the money is not ready, they expect to find food for themselves, procured at the expense of the Government, as that is part of their treaty. As soon as they are paid they leave, and very few are ever seen until the next year has past away. Last June they came in at the usual time, although many knew they should not come until were sent for, as before mentioned. But they were all in, and it was no use trying to send them back again, and of course they must live; and the prairie is a very poor place to find any kind of game, and five thousand people could not long stay where they were without something to support nature. When dried meat they brought was soon eaten, and in a few weeks they were absolutely starving; the children gathering and eating all kinds of green fruit, until the bushes were left bare. They had several councils, asking for food, which they did not get. Many days these poor creatures subsisted on a tall grass which they find in the marshes, chewing the roots, and eating the wild turnip. They would occasionally shoot a musk rat, and with what begging they would do, contrive to steal enough so they could live; but I know that many died from starvation or disease caused by improper food. It made my heart ache to see these creatures, and many times gave them food when I knew I was injuring ourselves pecuniarly; but I always felt as if they were God's creatures, and knew it was my duty to do all I could for them. I remember distinctly of the Agent giving them dry corn, and these poor creatures were so near starvation that they ate it raw, like cattle. They could not wait to cook it, and it affected them in such a manner that they were obliged to remove their camp to a clean spot of earth. This I witnessed. It is no idle story, and it is one of many scenes I witnessed during my short stay among them. I often wonder how these poor deceived creatures bore so much and so long without retaliation. People blame me for having sympathy for these creatures, but I take this view of the case: suppose the same number of whites were living in the sight of food, purchased with their own money, and their children dying of starvation, how long, think ye, would they remain quiet? I know of course, they would have done differently, but we must remember that the Indian is a wild man and has not the discrimination of a civilized person. When the Indian *wars*, it is blood for blood. They felt as if all whites were equally to blame. I do not wish anyone to think I uphold Indians in their murderous work. I should think I was insane, as many persons have said I was. I wish every murderer hanged; but those poor men who were dragged into this through fear, I pity, and think ought to be spared.

When on my way home from the lower Agency, the soldiers passed us on their return to Fort Ridgley. I was much surprised, and expressed my regret that they should leave so soon, and felt that was a very unwise proceeding; but the Captain assured us there was no longer any need of them, as the Indians had all departed.

That night the Agent had a war meeting, and a company of volunteers were raised, taking about forty men away, the Agent putting his name down first. They left in a few days, passed through the lower Agency, causing the Indians assembled at that place to think their "Great Father" had not many men left or he would not have taken them away from the Agency. They were very angry because the Agent did not stop and have a council with them, and give them goods and provisions, like the upper Indians. There has always been a jealousy among them, as they thought the upper Indians were better treated than they, and this feeling, with what the traders told them, exasperated these men, for they were suffering nearly as much as the Upper Indians. The traders said to them they would get no more money; that the Agent was going away to fight, and they would have to eat grass like cattle, etc.

The Indians always blamed the Agent for not giving them their goods, and repeatedly said if he had done so they would have scattered back to their homes satisfied, and this awful massacre would not have occurred; but he was deceived respecting these men. He thought they were just like white men, and would not dare rise, living as near as they did to the Fort; but he must now see his mistake in not explaining matters to these Indians; for only two or three days passed before they commenced their murderous work. I don't think he did this willingly; it was through ignorance. He did not understand the nature of the people he had in his charge.

Sunday, the 17th of August, the Indians killed some people in Acton, and on returning to Little Crow's village, said to him, what shall we do? He said they should go to the traders, kill them and all other whites; that they must clear the country of the whites so they might live. Monday, the 18th, they began their work of destruction at an early hour, killing traders in their stores; when this was done they began the work of destruction in general. The wine and spirits found in the stores added drunken madness to the madness of despairing vengeance, and soon the Indians were dancing wildly about the dying embers of what had lately been the stores and homes of the traders; then they passed on, killing everything they met. Their savage natures were aroused, and bloodthirsty as wild beasts, raced and tore around, beating, crushing and burning everything they had no use for.

Soon the news came that the soldiers were approaching, when they started for the ferry; but that bloody battle has been many times described, where so many of our kindred were murdered by these savage fiends, made so by liquor and revenge. This affair at the ferry seemed to cheer these people on, and they soon spread over the country, murdering all that were within their reach. How these savage creatures abused the traders after death is not generally known. They broke open the safe at the store and commenced pelting the dead bodies with gold, filling their mouths and ears, saying to them you have stole our money, now take all you will. Some of the Indians acted quite decently, and buried many things belonged to the missionaries, to save them from destruction. Monday, soon after dinner, my husband came in and said I had better get ready to go down to Fort Ridgely that afternoon, instead of waiting for the stage. Mr. Gleason had come up on Saturday and wished to return and had no conveyance, and had offered to drive me and the children to the Fort if my husband would let him take our horses and wagon. (Mr. Gleason was clerk in the ware house at the lower Agency.) At two o'clock we started. I felt unusually sad. I remember of going from room to room, taking a final look. My husband grew impatient and asked me what I was doing, and I made some excuse. I knew he would ridicule me if I told him how I felt. As we were starting he said, "Gleason, drive fast, so as to get to the Fort early." I asked what was the hurry, but he made me some answer that satisfied me then, but many times while I was in captivity I thought of our conversation. I inquired of Mr. Gleason if he had a pistol; he said he had, but it was not so; for after his death no weapons of any kind were found upon him. We drove to the traders, and Mr. Garvie came to the wagon and said he had heard the bad news; that the Indians had been killing some persons over in the "Big Woods," and that the Indians had been getting ugly, and at the lower Agency they were having councils to decide whether they should kill the whites, or if they should give up this country and leave for Red River. He also said that our Indians were only five miles away and were having councils to decide upon the same subject.

I was anxious to go back, as we were only under the hill from the hill from the Agency, but Mr. Gleason made great sport of me. He said he had no doubt that the upper Indians would make trouble and he was in a hurry to get home, for he would send four or five hundred lower Indians up to fight for the whites. He then told me that my husband had heard these reports, and this was his object in sending me away in such a hurry; that as soon as we got away from Yellow Medicine all would be right. Poor misguided man. All this day these lower Indians had been committing these awful murders, and we, not knowing it, were going down into their country for safety. I rode in great fear that afternoon. I was very sad and sorrowful. Death seemed hovering near me. Not a person or a living object did we meet as we rode, and I remarked to Mr. Gleason many times that there was something wrong below, as usually we were constantly meeting teams on that road.

Mr. Gleason was very lively, more so than I ever knew him. He would laugh, sing, shout, and when I would chide him and tell him how I felt, he would say I was nervous, and told me he would never take me anywhere again. I endeavored to have him return with me, but he said I would live to see the time I would thank him for taking me away. He tried every possible way to make me feel contented; but it was no use. I had strong feelings of evil, and it was a presentiment of what was to happen. As we got to the mound which is half way between the two Agencies, we could see distinctly the smoke of the burning buildings. I said to him that the Indians were destroying the Agency. "Oh, no: it is the saw mill or the prairie on fire." I became frightened, and tried again to persuade him to return. I was so excited I could not sit still, and endeavored to jump out of the wagon. Then he really scolded me, saying it was very unpleasant for him to have me act that way. Very well, said I, go on; they will not kill me; but they will shoot you, and take me prisoner. Why, said he, who are you talking about? The lower Indians are just like white men; you must not act so hysterical; for I was now crying. Very soon we came in sight of Mr. Reynolds' house, which was near the Redwood river, twenty-two miles from Yellow Medicine. He said to me, you now see you have been acting very foolishly, for "Old Joe's" house is standing. But for all, I could not look up or around only at that great body of smoke. As we drove towards the house he looked at his watch, and said "It is now quarter past six; we will eat supper here at "Old Joe's, " and at eight o'clock we will be at Fort Ridgely." The words had barely passed his lips, when, as we were descending a little hill, I saw two Indians coming towards us. I said, "Mr. Gleason, take out your pistol;" but he said "Be quiet, they are only boys going hunting." I then said hurry up your horses; instead of doing so he drew in the lines, and spoke to them, asking where they were going.

I will here describe the wagon we were in, and the way we were sitting. It was an open wagon with two seats. Mr. Gleason was sitting on the front seat, directly before me, my boy sitting at my right hand, my baby in my lap. And as the Indians passed the wagon, I turned my head, being suspicious, and just then one of them fired, the charge striking Mr. Gleason in his right shoulder, whereupon he fell backwards into my lap, crushing my baby against me. He did not speak, and immediately the savage fired again, striking him in his bowels as he laid across my lap. He now fell backwards out of the wagon as he turned at the first fire, bringing his back towards the side of the wagon. Oh! what a sight was that for a mother! and what were my thoughts, for I supposed I would be shot very soon! As he fell, the horses ran furiously, and the Indian who did not fire ran and caught the horses. As he came up, he asked me if I was the Doctor's wife. I said I was. He then said, "Don't talk much; that man," (pointing to the one that had shot Mr. Gleason,) "is a bad man. He has too much whiskey." As soon as he had quieted the horses, he came to the wagon and shook hands with us, and one ray of hope entered my heart; but it was soon dispelled, for when we turned around where poor Gleason lay groaning and writhing in his death agonies, I saw the other Indian loading his gun, and I expected every instant to be launched into eternity. When we rode up near, I begged him to spare me for my children's sake, and promised to sew, wash, cook, cut wood, anything rather than to die and leave my children. But he would not speak, only scowl hideously—Chaska, the good man, urging me by his looks to be quiet. Just then Mr. Gleason spoke for the first time, saying: "Oh my God, Mrs. Wakefield!" when Hapa, the savage one, fired again, killing him instantly. He stretched out and became calm without a groan. Now, as I write it, all appears plain before me, and I can scarcely hold my pen. I never can feel worse than I did that night. I passed through death many times in imagination during my stay on that prairie. It now seems so plain before me I cannot keep from trembling; but it must be told. In a moment after poor Gleason breathed his last, Hapa stepped up to the wagon and taking aim at my head, would have killed me but for Chaska, who leaped towards him and struck the gun out of his hands. I begged Hapa to spare me, put out my hands towards him, but he struck them down. I thought then my doom was sealed, and if it had not been for Chaska, my bones would now be bleaching on that prairie, and my children with Little Crow. Three or four times did this demon try to destroy me, when Chaska would draw him away with his arm, and I could hear him tell him of some little act of kindness my husband or myself had shown them in years gone by. But all Hapa would say, was, "She must die; all whites are bad, better be dead." Who can imagine my feelings, exposed as I was to the danger of being shot every moment, and not knowing that might be my fate if I was spared.

I think those men disputed about me nearly an hour. Chaska trying every inducement to influence him in my favor. How many and varied were my thoughts. I felt as if death was nothing, if my children were dead; but to die and leave my petted ones to the fate that might be in store for them was agony. I could see them left to starve to death, or partly murdered, lying in agony calling for their dead mother. Father in Heaven, I pray you impress this upon the minds of an ungenerous world, who blame me for trying to save the man who rescued me from death when it was very near! After a long time, Hapa consented I should live, after inquiring very particularly if I was the Agent's wife. He thought I was; but Chaska knew to the contrary, for he had been at my house in Shakopee many times. He often said that if Hapa could have got the Agent's wife, he would have cut her to pieces, on her husband's account.

Chaska and Hapa got into the wagon, leaving poor Gleason on that prairie alone with his God. Unfortunate man! If he only had listened to my entreaties, his life might have been saved, and I been spared six weeks of painful captivity. I rode in much agony; I knew not where I was to be taken, or what might eventually be my fate. I turned and took a last took at Mr. Gleason's remains; his hat was slouched over his face, his dog looking pitifully at him, and just as the sun went down, I bid farewell to him forever, Chaska telling me not to look any more, for Hapa was very cross, and said if I turned around he would kill me now.

Hapa sat facing me all the way, pointing his gun at my breast; and he kept saying, "Those children I will kill; they will be a trouble when we go to Red River." But Chaska said, "No, I am going to take care of them; you must kill me before you can any of them." Chaska was a farmer Indian, and had worn white man's dress for several years; had been to school and could speak some English, and read and spell very little.

Hapa was a wild "Rice Creek Indian," a horrid, blood-thirsty wretch, and here can be seen the good work of the Missionaries. The two men were vastly different, although they both belonged to one band and one family; but the difference was this: the teaching that Chaska had received; although he was not a Christian, he knew there was a God, and he had learned right from wrong.

After riding a few miles, we reached the Indian encampment, consisting of about two hundred persons. As they perceived who I was, their laments were really touching to my feelings. They proved to be old friends of mine. Six years previous to my living at the Agency, I had lived in the town of Shakopee. In the winter there were camped around the town this same band that I was now among. Not a day passed but some of the Indians were at my house, and I had always pitied them, and given them food. But at the time of the battle between the Chippewas and the Sioux, near Shakopee, many Sioux were wounded, and my husband attended them, extracting bullets, etc., and they often said he saved many of their lives; and now I was with them they said they would protect me and mine. When they assisted me in alighting, many of the old squaws cried like children. They spread down carpets for me to sit on, gave me a pillow, and wished me to lie down and rest. They prepared my supper, and tried every way possible to make me comfortable; but that was an impossibility. They promised me life, but I dared not hope, and felt as if death was staring me in the face.

I had not been there long when a half-breed approached, saying he felt very sorry to see me, and that I would probably be spared a few days, but would at last be killed, as they had sworn to kill everyone that had white blood in their veins. He did very wrong, for he knew better than try to increase my fears. He was a great rogue.

After the old squaws had given my children supper, Chaska said I had better go with him to a house where there was another white woman, for my children would take cold sleeping on the prairie, as they would not put up their tepees that night. I was afraid to go, and I asked the half-breed what I had better do. He advised me to go; he said Chaska was a good man, and you can trust him, and you will be better treated. He gave me some very good advice. Said as long as I was with them I must try to be pleased, and not mistrust them; make them think I had confidence in them, and they would soon learn to love and respect me, and that would be my only way of prolonging my life.

I started on with Chaska, leaving my trunk of clothing in the wagon, carrying my baby and leading my little boy; Chaska carrying my satchel. We walked about a mile, part of the way through the woods. I was suspicious, but I kept up with him, and tried to talk of the heavy dew which was falling, not letting him know I was frightened. He stopped at a tepee, I suppose to show his prisoner; and while I was there the Indians brought in Mr. Gleason's clothes, and his watch, which was running. I looked at it and saw it was just eight o'clock, the very hour he said we would be at Fort Ridgely. The crystal was broken in the center, with a bullet I expect. The Indians were having great sport over his empty pockets. He had no pistol, and deceived me. It was not safe any time to go without fire-arms, and I many times wonder why he did such an unwise thing. There was a white woman in this tepee. I did not learn her name. She was a German, and her greatest trouble seemed to be the loss of her feather beds. She had seen her husband killed, but that was very little compared with her other losses. They asked me to take off my hoops, which I did. I think I should have cut off my right hand if I could have saved my life by so doing. We only stayed there a short time, and then went to a bark house where I found another German woman. They had a good fire, plenty of candles, and made me as good a bed as could be expected. I was told to lie down and go to sleep, as we would start for Red River in the morning; but sleep was far away from our eyelids that night and many others. After Chaska had made us comfortable, he left us in charge of some old squaws and boys, telling me to go to his mother's tepee in the morning, and tell her to give me a squaw dress, saying I would be more safe in such an attire. The German woman and I managed to get through the night, but she spoke very poor English; still she was white.

No one can imagine the confusion of an Indian camp when the braves come home victorious; it is like Bedlam broken loose. Hour after hour we sat listening to every footstep, expecting death every minute. Guns were firing in all directions, women were mourning over their dead, and the conjurors were at work over the sick and wounded, all tending to increase the confusion.

Morning came at last, and as the sun arose, the Indians began to leave us. They were going to attack Fort Ridgely. Now as it was quiet, I went to Chaska's mother, and soon I was changed from a white woman to a squaw. How humiliating it was to adopt such a dress even forced by such circumstances. This day, Tuesday the 19th, was an extremely hot day, and I began to suffer. My bonnet was gone, as well as everything I possessed. I thought I would be sun struck, for we were kept on a constant move. The squaws would get frightened, pack up, and off we would go; when soon they would hear different stories and we would rest awhile. Many, many times that day, was that repeated. Once they heard the Sissetons, or upper Indians, were coming, when the old woman rubbed dirt in my skin to make me look more like a squaw. Surely I did not look like a white woman. I had the pleasure of viewing myself, for they had a large glass belonging to Mrs. Reynolds resting against the fence, and the squaws were having a fine time admiring themselves.

I sat down by the roadside, and while we were waiting for news from the Fort, I tried to disguise my children. I rubbed dirt all over my boy, but his white hair would betray him. I tore off the skirt of my baby's dress, took off her shoes and stockings, but did not rub dirt into her flesh, for she is naturally of a very dark skin, and the squaws said she looked like a papoose after I had made her ragged.

During the morning, an old squaw called Lightfoot came and sat down by me, and said they were going to kill me in a few days, but were going to keep my children, and when they were large, their Great Father would give them much money for them. I became nearly frantic. I had thought of this all night, and I determined I would kill them rather than leave them with those savages. I ran to a squaw, begged her knife and caught up my little girl, and in a moment I would have cut her throat, when a squaw said it was false. What I suffered, let every mother imagine, when you think of my trying to cut my child's throat myself. But my thoughts were always like this: if my children were only dead and out of trouble I could die willingly, for I supposed my husband was dead and I cared to live only for my children.

About four o'clock in the afternoon, Chaska's mother came into her lodge saying that a man was coming to kill me, and she caught up Nellie, my baby, on her back and told me and my boy to hurry. She stopped at the bark house where I had stayed the night before; told an old man her story, and he said flee to the woods. She gave me a bag of crackers and a cup and we ran to a ravine; it was very steep, the banks were like the roof of a house; when we got to the bottom she hid me in tall grass and underbrush, and bidding me sit still, left me, saying she would come in the morning.

I have passed through many trials and different scenes, but never suffered as I did then. God so willed it that a storm arose as the sun went down, and a furious storm it was. No one, unless a Minnesotian, can judge our thunder showers. But I did not fear the storm. I felt God had sent the storm for my benefit; still we suffered from the effects of it. The rain and mud washed down upon us from the side of the hill, wetting us completely through in a few minutes. I had one blanket and tried to keep my children covered with that. I had in my satchel a small bottle of brandy, and I put it into my bosom, and during that night, as my children would awaken, I would give them some in their drink; it kept them from taking cold. When I recall that night my heart beats with fear. Surely God gave me strength or I would have died through fear, for I am by nature a very cowardly woman; every leaf that fell during that night was a footstep, and every bough that cracked was the report of a gun. My nerves were so weakened that my heart beats would sound like some one running, and I would frequently hold my breath to listen. Muskrats looked like wolves, and as they crawled around me in the darkness, I thought they were wolves, and they were going to devour me. I sat all night, my feet in a running brook, and I dared not stir for fear I might make some noise that would lead to my discovery; for I could hear the Indians racing around, firing guns, singing, hooting and screaming. Many persons who may read this may think I was foolish in giving away to my fears, but you cannot tell what you would do or how you would feel; for I many times now, when I think of it, think I was very foolish; still I have no doubt I should feel the same under the like circumstances. My children would awaken often, and I would hush them, telling them the Indians were near, when the little darlings would lay close to me and tremble with fear. I cannot tell how I lived through that night, but I know God was with me. I passed the time in prayer. I thought of my husband lying murdered in his blood, and my friends in a like manner; then I would beg God if they were alive to spare them. I know he heard me, for we all know how narrowly they escaped.

After a flash of lightning I would pray for the next to strike me, or else save me to meet my husband. I never knew how to pray before; but I had no one to call upon but God, and I knew He could save me, and I begged and plead with Him all that night, as a child would with a father. Never can I forget His goodness; never can I cease praying to One who brought me out of such dangers.

Morning came at last. Sorry was I to see the light. I felt sure we would now be discovered and our fate sealed. Hour after hour passed, still the old woman came not, and it was all quiet where noise had prevailed during the night; nothing could be heard but the singing of the birds or the running of the brook.

I now began to think she had forgotten me and removed, and that my children and myself would be left to perish in the ravine. I knew I could not climb those banks alone, and our bag of crackers would not last long; and I now saw starvation, as well as other evils, staring us in the face. Our situation was horrible. We were completely covered with mud, and now the sun was shining, the mosquitoes were very numerous. My childrens faces were running with blood from their bites, but the darlings were as quiet as if they had been at ease, for their fears were so great they did not notice their stings.

After waiting several hours I saw the old woman coming, and I was overjoyed to see her. We laughed, cried, and I really think I kissed her, for I felt as if our deliverer had now come. She took Nellie on her back, and I tried to get up, for found I could not stand, from the effects of sitting so long in one position; and my limbs in the water had chilled my blood and stopped my circulation. But the old woman rubbed me and while doing so said the men had gone who were going to kill me, and I must try to walk to her tepee, when she would give me some dry clothes and some coffee. She said they had removed across the Redwood river, and this accounted for the stillness in the morning.

When I was able to walk we started, she carrying both children up the bank, and then helped me up, for I had not strength to get up alone. I was completely prostrated; I had not eaten a morsel since I left home on Monday; now it was Wednesday. The exposure and fright, combined with nursing a child twenty months old, had reduced my strength exceedingly. When we got to the bark house, the old woman got me a cup of coffee and some pain-killer, which revived me greatly. We walked for about three miles, stopping at every tepee for a cup of coffee or tea; and she would make me sit down and warm myself, for I was shivering with fear and disease.

At last we came to the Redwood river, and we commenced fording it, the water in some places being up to my shoulders—the old woman still carrying my baby, and I my boy, where he could not walk. But the child was as brave as a man, and ran along through the woods that morning with scarce a murmur, the bushes tearing his little bare feet until the blood ran; occasionally he would exclaim "Oh! Oh!" I would shake my head and speak in Dakota, that the Indians would hear him, when he would remain quiet, when I knew the little creature was suffering extremely, for I could not bear my own suffering without a groan occasionally.

We did not go in paths or roads, but through the tallest and thickest brush, and among all kinds of berry bushes entwined together, with grape vines and ivy; we did not stop even to part them, but tore through like wild beasts when driven by fear, and of course we tore our flesh badly. I am completely covered with scars which I will carry to my grave.

Those persons who think I prefer Indian life to civilized, ought to travel as I did last summer. It was because I was carried through so much by that family to save me from death; and what is more, that I was anxious to do all I possibly could for them when they needed assistance.

After crossing the river we arrived safely at their encampment. They had no tepees up, but were getting dinner, each family by their wagon.

When I came to where my home was to be, I felt comparatively happy. I had endured so much the past night that even squaws seemed like friends, and they proved to be good, true friends. Poor women! How I pity many of them; driven from good homes, their families broken up and divided. Many of them are as much to be pitied as the whites, and many of them no more to blame.

When I rested awhile, they gave me my dinner, dry clothes, water to wash my children, and prepared me a bed to lie down.

I feared that Chaska was still absent; that he and his mother were living with Hapa and his wife, she being a half sister of Chaska. Her name was Winona, and I feared her, for she was like her husband, the murderer of poor Gleason. She tried every way to make me unhappy when Chaska was absent, but was very good in his presence. I will here say that my trunk of clothing, which was very valuable, she appropriated to her own use and would not give us anything to wear; and the old woman would go around and beg when my children needed a change of clothing. She took my ear rings from my ears and put tin ones in their place, and dressed herself in mine; cut up my silk dresses and made her boys coats to tumble around in the dirt with. All little articles, like minatures, etc., she would destroy before me, and would laugh when she saw I felt sad. I would like to be her judge, if she is ever brought within my reach. She and her husband are now with Little Crow.

After lying quiet about an hour, I was surrounded by squaws, who commenced talking about some evil that threatened me. The old woman said there was a bad man who would kill me, and I had better go to the woods again. I told her I could not, and must die, for I was completely exhausted. I arose and looked north where the excitement was, and I saw a hut made of green boughs, and women led into it by an Indian wearing a white band on his head; presently I would hear a shriek and see female clothing spread out, and what we all thought were bodies put into an ox wagon, and then driven off. A German, (the only man who was spared, except George Spear,) came where I was hidden under the wagon, and said we were all to be killed in a short time. He said the squaws were much excited, and wished him to hide in the woods, but he thought it was useless. The old woman soon came back, and said, "You must not talk, and I'll cover you and your boy up with buffalo robes and the tepee cloth," and then taking my baby again on her back, kept marching backwards and forwards, as if she was guarding me.

I had made up my mind to die. I knew if Chaska was only near he would save me, but I had not seen him since the night I was taken prisoner. I conversed with my boy in a whisper, charging him to try to remember his name and his sister's, and tried to impress upon him the necessity of always staying with her and taking care of her, so that if his father or uncle should be alive, he might some day be able to find them.

Several times I raised the cloth and inquired what the news was, but the woman was crying, and would only say, "Chaska dead, and you will die soon; that man is a very bad man." I cannot describe my feelings. I know I prayed; that I begged God to save me from the savages; sometimes I cried, then I would be calm, and once I began to sing. I thought I would not die despairing; I would try and go to my death cheerfully. At last I felt perfectly happy, and I believe if I had died then, I would have died a Christian. I had bidden the world farewell. My husband I thought was dead, and all I had to live for was my children, and I was in hopes they might go with me. I said to my little boy, who was not quite five years of age, "James, you will die and go to heaven." "Oh! mamma! I am glad, ain't you? for my father is there, and I will take him this piece of bread," (which he was eating.) Poor child! he was not old enough to realize how he was to reach that happy land.

I asked Winona how we were to be killed, and she said "Stabbed," pointing near the heart. I dreaded death in that way, for I was fearful we might suffer for some time. When I sat there thinking of my sad fate and of my friends in the East, and how they would feel when they heard of my death, I thought I heard a neigh from our mare that Chaska had gone away on. Soon I heard her mate, who was tied near, respond, and I felt a sudden thrill, as if my preserver had come. In a moment the tepee cloth was raised and Winona said, "Come out; Chaska has come, it is all right now." I did not need a second invitation. I went out and surely there he stood. He shook hands, and said "Don't be afraid; he will not dare to hurt you while I am near; if he comes near I will shoot him." Oh! how happy was I. My life was again saved, and by him. Had not God raised me up a protector among the heathen? Have I not reason to bless his name, and thank the man and his family for all their goodness towards me and mine? for my children would now be motherless if he had not taken care of me.

The remainder of this day I passed quietly. That night a violent hurricane arose, upsetting our tepee, which had been put up soon after Chaska arrived, and we were compelled to go under the wagon and lie down on the wet grass the remainder of the night, while the rain poured down upon us. Thursday, the twenty-first of August, the Indians were up very early, getting ready for an attack upon the Fort. Chaska was going, and said he was afraid to leave us where we were, for fear Hapa might return and kill us. He told me I had better go with him to his old grandfather's who lived in a brick house about a mile from where we were. Soon the wagon was ready, and myself and children and the old woman were riding away. Before leaving, Winona painted my cheeks and a part of my hair. She tied my hair (which was braided like a squaw's down my back) with several colored ribbons, and ornamented me with fancy colored leggins, moccasins, etc. My children were painted in a like manner; then she gave me a blanket and told me to start. Who would have known me to be a white woman? I sometimes forgot I was, when I would look around me and see how I was living. If I had been without children I should not have stayed there and submitted to being painted and dressed in such a manner. I should have tried to escape, and if I had died in that attempt, well and good; I should have had no children to leave. As it was I dared not try, for I knew I would be discovered and then death would have been certain.

The prairie that morning was alive with Indians all in high spirits, and confident of taking Fort Ridgely. They were either over-dressed *or else not dressed at all;* their horses were covered with ribbons, bells, or feathers, all jingling, tinkling as we rode along, the Indians singing their war songs. It was a grand but savage sight to see so many great powerful men mounted on their bedecked animals, going to war. Many of the men were entirely naked with the exception of the breech cloth, their bodies painted and ridiculously ornamented. I little thought one week before when passing over that road, that I should be in such a train, and the train on its way to kill my kindred. We arrived at the house of his grandfather just at sunrise; it was a very cool morning, and a fire which they had in the stove cooking breakfast, was really comfortable. There were several tepees around his house. I found, after alighting from the wagon, that I was with some of my best friends in the Shakopee band. An old squaw called by the whites, "Mother Friend," was there, and glad was I to see her. Chaska went soon after I got my breakfast, saying he would stop for us at night. I passed this day in great anxiety; we could hear the cannon at the Fort, and see the smoke from the burning buildings. We heard many different stories relative to the fight; sometimes we would hear the Indians were all killed and that the whites were coming; then the confusion that would ensue was such, that many times we fled to the ravines and hid ourselves in the bushes.

The squaws were very cowardly and I was needlessly frightened many times by them. My children feasted this day, one family having enough nuts, candy, maple sugar, &c., to open a confectionary store.

I never shall forget the kindness of old Mother Friend that day; she would not let me stay in the old man's house, but must pass the day with her. She made my boy new moccasins, brought water and washed my sacque, carried my baby around on her back, and did all in her power to lighten my sufferings. She said when the old grandmother came to dinner, "No, she is my child, she has given me cooked food in her tepee in Shakopee; now she must stay and eat bread with me." Her daughters tried every way to amuse me, and would tell me that when their father came home, he would take me down the river in a boat, but although the father was kind, he never offered to take me down as they promised.

Just at sun set a messenger arrived, saying the Indians were going to stay all night, and that a chief was coming to kill us white women, there being two besides myself in that camp. I was told to flee to the woods again, and Eagle Head, Chaska's grandfather, said he would go with me. He was an old man, nearly eighty years old. Mother Friend said I should leave James, as he was asleep, and she would take care of him. The old man took his gun, and I my baby on my back; we started in great haste for the woods, which we roamed all night from dark until daylight, never stopping only

long enough to nurse my baby; when we would hear them shouting, and would dive deeper into the gloom. The old man could not
keep up with me, but I would wait for him, and he would say,
"Stop, I am tired; I will die." As the day began at dawn, it became
quiet, and we came out of the woods on the bottom lands of the
Minnesota river. He said he would go back to camp, but he must
hide me first, for he dared not take me back until he know how
matters were. He proposed hiding me in a hay stack, saying he
would pull out the centre and put me in the middle and then cover
me up. He did so and left me to sit as I thought for a short time;
but hour after hour passed. It was noon, and I thought I would
suffocate or die of thirst. My baby kept worrying for we started
without supper, and the child was hungry; while she was nursing
it would pacify her, but made me very weak, for not having eaten
anything, I had very little to nurse her. I sat hours that day nursing her, when I thought I should faint with the constant drain
upon me. I could hear water running but dared not come out of
my hiding place, for I had seen Indians very near me twice that
day. I nearly choked my child when I heard the Indians coming,
and she was fretting; I clasped my hand around her throat until
she was black in her face, for I knew her cries would lead to our
discovery and death. Poor baby, she thought her mamma very
unkind, for she would look so pitifully when I would do so, but it
saved out lives.

I sat there that way all day, until sunset. I thought night would
never come. I was miserable on account of my boy. I knew he
would cry himself sick, for he never was away from me a night in

his life. How I blamed myself for leaving him, but I expected when I left to return in a few hours. Where, Oh! where was my child, I would ask myself. I was fearful he would scream and cry and some ugly Indian would kill him. Soon after sunset I heard a voice and footstep near, but I dared not speak. Presently the old white head of Chaska's grandfather appeared, and he said, "Come out," at the same time throwing the hay off me. I was rejoiced to see the old man. He said I must not talk loud for some of the Indians were ugly. I asked for drink or food—he said I must wait until I got to the tepee. It was sometime before I was able to stand, as I had sat in one position eighteen hours with my feet drawn up under me. As soon as I could stand, we started and I found we had got to walk several miles. I did not think I could live to walk but strength was given me.

I inquired for my boy but he knew nothing about him. All the gloomy thoughts I had indulged in during the day arose in my mind, and I was almost sure he must be dead, or he would know where he was; still I knew Mother Friend would save him if possible.

As we walked along we passed through a muddy piece of ground, and I dipped up the filthy water in my hands and drank and gave my child. It was refreshing, but I think a dog would refuse to drink such water in ordinary times, but my mouth was parched with thirst. Many times during the day I reached my hand into the middle of the hay stack and would find some moist hay, and draw it through my lips to try to moisten that awful dryness of my mouth and throat.

We walked I think four miles; every one I met I inquired

about my child, but could hear nothing of him. I at last arrived at the tepee. He was not there, but Winona soon came in saying that he was very near. Presently he came in; what a joyful moment for a mother's heart. He rushed into my arms and cried if his little heart would break, "Oh, mamma, I thought you was dead, and I was left alone with the Indians. I have cried until I am sick. Oh dear mamma have you got back? Do kiss me, and keep your arms around me. I thought you and Nellie had gone to heaven and left your boy all alone." He said he did not awake until morning, and Mother Friend told him I would be back soon. After he had his breakfast, Winona came and carried him up to her tepee on her back. He said he had cried so much that Roy, a half breed, had taken him to see an ox killed, "But mamma, I thought you might be somewhere shot like the ox, and it made me cry some more."

I could not get him out of my arms that night. He clung to me in his sleep, and trembled with fear if I would make an attempt to lay him down. I sat all night and held him, and watched the stars through the opening of our tepee, and wondered if his father could see him and me in my captivity.

I learned after a while, that the Indian who threatened us came, and as were all secreted, they told him we were at the large encampment. They searched around and went to the woods, but it being dark, and they lazy and tired, concluded to wait until morning to put their threats into execution, which it appears, was not death, but what would have been even worse. Now, my readers, what say you? Am I not in debt to those friendly Indians for my life and honor? What would have been my lot that night if they had not interested themselves to save me, you can imagine. I can never express my gratitude to those who befriended me, when in such danger; let people blame me if they will, God, who knoweth all things, will judge me, and I will wait and bear all the reproaches that the world may cast upon me, knowing that with Him all will be well.

The next day being Saturday, we arose early, as it was reported we should leave for Yellow Medicine in course of the day. The morning passed quietly, the Indians deciding to remain until Tuesday. Soon after dinner, an Indian called Chaska out. He returned very soon saying, "I wish I could kill all the Indians." I inquired what was the trouble. He said an Indian was drunk in the next tepee and was going to shoot all the white women in our camp. He told his mother to close the teopa, or door, and watch; just then I heard the report of a gun and a woman shrieked, "I am shot! I am shot!" The old woman said he had shot her through the legs, as she sat outside the teepee.

Chaska appeared much alarmed. He sat down on the ground, told me to sit back of him, taking my children in my lap; and if the Indian came, he must shoot me through him before reaching me. We sat this way a long time, until his mother said, he had passed away from our tepee, when she tore up the back part of our tepee and taking Nellie on her back we again fled to the woods. She found a good place, covered us up with boughs of trees, and left in a hurry; did not say when she would return. I sat awhile and hearing running water I thought I would follow it, and perhaps I might reach the Minnesota river. I took Nellie on my back (as I had learned to carry her in that fashion,) and we followed the brook some ways, until a large tree which had fallen across it completely impeded our progress. I was obliged to stop and retrace my steps, and I decided to remain, as it was a very good hiding place. We then sat in the water until sunset, when I heard the old woman calling, "White woman! Where are you?" She had been where she had left us and was much frightened when she found us gone. She followed our tracks along the stream, and appeared to be delighted to see us again. I am sure I was rejoiced to see her honest old face, and as she took my baby again on her back and arranged my blanket over my shoulders, and scattered my hair over my face to conceal my countenance, I could not refrain from giving her a good kiss. I learned to look upon that woman as I would upon a mother, and I hope some day to be able to do something for her. She said a large number of Indians had just come in from the Fort, bringing many mules, and that now was a favorable opportunity for me to go back home, as they were so excited over their plunder. We were near our tepee, when she discovered the Indian we were in fear of, and she hurried me into a tepee and covered me up with robes, telling me to lie as quiet and as flat as I could; then the squaws threw their packages on to me, and I looked like a great bundle of goods. The old woman left, telling the squaws to give the children food. Soon some Indians came in and asked whose children they were. They said their father and mother were dead. I expected my boy would speak and say who he was, for he could speak Dakota very well, but the child showed the good sense and reason of a man all the time we were in captivity. In a few minutes the very Indian who had threatened me, came and inquired if a white woman was there. They said no. I can assure all that may read this, that my heart beat with fear and trembling, for I did not know these squaws, and did not know but they might betray me. While I lay there, an Indian lad came in and sat down on me, thinking I was a bundle of goods piled up against the tepee. Fortunately he sat only a short time, or I think I should have been smothered. I could not take a long breath for fear he would notice the motion of my body. Soon Winona came in and told me to hurry back; we went home and had a good supper, and glad I was to lie down and rest, for my feet had become so sore that I could hardly walk, and they were very painful; my left foot was entirely covered with sores, poisoned by weeds, and constantly irritated by running through the prairie grass.

I always felt safe when I was in Chaska's tepee, for he always cautioned me when he went away not to go out unless I was obliged to, saying that no man dared enter the tepee of another person and commit any violence, unless it was a drunken person. There was no need of cautioning me, for I had no disposition to run around, for I had traveling enough that was necessary. Many of the white prisoners were roving from morning until night, and would often wish me to accompany them, but I always refused. I could not be happy in any place, and if I could sit with the old woman and have her wash my feet and attend to my sores, it was all I cared for. I felt as if this was my home, and I stayed there all the time I was in captivity, and was treated much better than any other female on that account.

I thought I was better off staying there attending to my children than I was in roving around gossiping, all the time in danger of being shot down by Indian soldiers, for of all the places for gossip I ever was in, the Indian camp was the worst. Last summer there were many half-breeds who spoke good English, that repeated every word spoken by us white women, to the Indians, and so things were exaggerated and misconstrued, going through so many lips and different languages. I always took particular pains to speak in favor of the Indians, many times upholding them in their undertakings, because I knew it would all be repeated again to the Indians; and my sole object while there was to gain their friendship so as to save my life, hoping that God would pardon me for any deceit used in such a way. I little thought every word would be remembered and told to my injury. I trust God may forgive those that have done this grievous wrong, as fully as I do; for the worst is for themselves.

Saturday night I slept very well until near midnight, when Hapa came home, the first time since my captivity. He was drunk, as usual. He awakened all by his drunken actions, but I little thought of his daring to molest me in the tepee in the presence of all the family. I pretended to be asleep, but soon he asked where the white woman was. He said, "Come here, I wish to talk with you." I dared not speak or move; I thought now he will kill me, as a drunken Indian knows not what he is doing. I asked the old woman in a whisper what I should do; she said, "Lie still, Chaska will not let him hurt you; he will go to sleep soon." But not he, for he soon rose and, with a knife drawn, came towards my place saying, "You must be my wife or die." I said, "Chaska, come here he will kill me." He said, "Be still; I will take care of you;" whereupon he arose and came towards me, asking Hapa what he wanted. He said, "She must be my wife or die." Chaska said, "You are a bad man; there is your wife, my sister. I have no wife, and I don't talk bad to white women." I told Chaska to let him kill me, only kill my children first. He said, "Stop talking then." He turned to Hapa, who had his knife drawn and still flourishing it, and said, "You go lie down; I will take her for my wife, for I have none." He said, "That is right, you take her, and I will not kill her." Chaska said, "Yes, as soon as I know her husband is dead, I will marry her;" but Hapa said I must be his (Chaska's) wife immediately. I did not know what to do. I caught hold of the old woman's hand, but she said, "Don't be afraid, Chaska is a good man; he will not injure you." Then Chaska said, "You must let me lie down beside you or he will kill you. He is so drunk. I am a good man, and my wife is in the 'spirit world,' and can see me, and I will not harm you." He came and laid down between his mother and me, and Hapa went back contented, and soon was in a deep, drunken slumber. When Chaska thought he was asleep he very quietly crawled back to his own place, and left me as he found me. My father could not have done differently, or acted more respectful or honorable; and if there was ever an upright, honest man, he was one. He suffered death, but God will reward him in heaven for his acts of kindness towards me. This was not the only time he saved me in a like manner. Very few Indians, or *even white men* would have treated me in the manner he did. I was in his power, and why did he not abuse me? because he knew that it was a sin; he knew I was a wife, and he always intended to restore me to my husband, and often said he would give me up as he took me.

It was constantly reported and many believed that I was his wife, and I dared not contradict it, but rather encouraged every one to believe so, for I was in fear all the while that Hapa would find out we had deceived him. I did not consider the consequences outside of the Indian camp, for I had my doubts all the while of my getting away. I supposed if I was ever so fortunate as to get back I could then explain all, never once thinking people would consider me a liar, as many call me. Mine is a sad case, after all I have passed through, to receive now so many reproaches from those that I thought would pity me.

Sunday morning our tepee blew down again, and we were obliged to sit under the wagon and wait for the old woman to go to the woods and cook our breakfast, for the wind was so high they could not cook on the prairie. I was visited this day by a number of white women, they said they had heard I was married, and asked me if that was my husband. I replied that my husband I expected was in heaven, and turned the conversation; for there were many near that could understand all we were talking about. These women went away and said I acknowledged it. Now this is the truth, and I am very sorry to say that women would do such a thing towards one of their own sex.

Sunday night I had been in bed, (or what was called my bed, consisting of two strips of carpeting, two blankets and two pillows,) when Chaska came in with two Indians I never saw before, and said I must take my children and go with him. I asked where, and what was the matter. He said he would sometime tell me. I got ready, awakened my children, and we started. I knew not what was in store for me, still I trusted him and went along. Chaska carried James and I Nellie, and the two strange Indians walked on each side as a guard. It was very dark; a drizzling rain was falling, and here was I at the mercy of these men, going I knew not whither: but as I had always found him truthful and honest, I could not feel as I might do otherwise. We walked a long way; and left our own encampment far behind us, and still we went on, and not a ray of light was visible. I began now to be suspicious, but he would only say, "Keep still." We at last came to a small encampment, and he took me to his aunt's tepee, and told her I should stay there. They whispered together sometime, and she looked at me very sadly. He left, saying he would come again in the morning. I never learned why I was carried there. I presume some danger threatened. Surely I was well watched and cared for by these people. Could white people do more?

The Indians were as respectful towards me as any white man would be towards a lady; and now, when I hear all the Indians abused, it aggravates me, for I know some are as manly, honest, and noble, as our own race. I remained at Chaska's aunt's, who was a widow, all the next day; towards night he came, and soon after his mother, and she said I must go, that the Indians were coming, and next morning we would certainly start for Yellow Medicine, on our way to Big Stone lake.

When we were going home, I saw an Indian who exclaimed, "There is the Doctor's wife." I smiled, and the old woman said,

"Hurry on, he is a Sisseton, and will kill you." I was not afraid, as I knew the Sissetons would take care of me, and longed to go to Yellow Medicine. I knew the Sisseton chiefs would never allow Little Crow to kill me. He was constantly threatening us all, and myself in particular. He was determined at times to destroy me, I being the only one of the Yellow Medicine people that fell into his hands; and he very often said I should die, because they escaped; this caused me more trouble than any other woman there.

I remembered one day, while I was still at Redwood, that a half-breed said there had been a council, and that all the whites would be killed very soon. I sent for Shakopee, the chief of the band I was with; and when he came, I asked him if I was to be killed; and I told him if he would only spare me that I would help kill the other prisoners, I also promised never to leave his band, and that I would sew, chop wood and be like a squaw. I was so frightened that I really did not know what I was saying, nor did I care; for all I thought of was, if I can only live a while longer, and get away, my husband, if living, will not care what promises I made, if his wife and children are saved.

It was awful the crazy promises I made to kill my own people, but I was nearly crazy, and was expecting the soldiers to come very soon, and wished to live to see them. Many unthinking captives, hearing me make such remarks, have since published it to the world, causing people to believe I really meant all I said. Being naturally timid, and afraid of death under any circumstances, I looked upon such a death with horror. One day the old woman seemed much worried about something. I could not understand what. Chaska was away. Soon I heard guns firing, and I imagined that they were shooting the white women. Now this I am about to write was all imagination, to show people how my mind was a great part of the time.

I sat under the wagon this day, and near us was an ox-wagon, and I sat there and watched that wagon all day, imagining that it was full of dead bodies, and there being buffalo robes over the bodies. I could not see them, but could see their long hair hanging from under the robes. In the course of the day Winona came in with a piece of skin, and I thought as she laid it up to dry, it was put around my throat, after it was cut. Now this was a piece of ox (the sinew) there were to sew with; and the hair that I thought was human, was from the buffalo robes. Such a day as I passed! I suffered as much as if it had been real. I often wonder that I was not entirely deranged.

The night before we started for Yellow Medicine there was little rest; the women were packing and the men were preparing for battle, as the report came that the soldiers were coming. Just as it got light they started. My boy was sick with bowel complaint. I was forced to take off his pants, and not having any others, he traveled without anything on except a shirt and a little waist that held his pants up.

I had no moccasins allowed me that day, for squaws go barefoot when traveling, and I must do likewise. Although they were in a great hurry, they did not neglect to paint my cheeks and ornament my hair. They were anxious to look fine, as they were going up into the Sisseton country. When the train started, in every direction, as far as the eye could reach, were Indians, all hurrying for the Redwood crossing. The old woman became much excited, and said I must hurry, as the Sissetons were coming and would kill me. That day I had my baby to carry, for the old woman had about eighty pounds to carry on her back. Such noise and confusion I never heard. My boy was crying, "I cannot walk so fast." Nellie would slip down nearly to my feet, and she would cry, and the old woman would fret because I could not keep her up on my back, squaw style. If I stopped she would scold, and say I must "Go on, go." When we got to the river we found it full of teams, some fast in the mud; here a horse floundering in the water, there a boy trying to regain his footing; then you might see a horse with poles attached and an old woman up to her knees striving to urge the beast through; but the noise and confusion excited beasts as well as men, and I was fearful we would be crushed to death, for the Indian soldiers were galloping in every direction firing their guns, not minding and not caring on what or where they tramped. Fortunately the river is not deep in the summer; if it had been many of us poor females would have drowned. We were all more or less wet. I had my baby on my back, my boy by my hand, and it was difficult endeavoring to keep myself from being drawn down by the current, for the water in many places was up to my shoulders, when I would have to take my boy in my arms, making quite a burden for a person not accustomed to such labor. When I was striving to get through an Indian rode up to me and asked, "Where are you going?" I replied, "To Yellow Medicine." He said, "You are the Doctor's wife?" I said, "No, I am an Indian woman," for the old woman just whispered, "He is a Sisseton." He laughed and said, "I know you; you must not tell lies; you are not an Indian woman, your eyes are too light." When we got up to the bank after crossing the river, where Mr. Reynolds' house once stood, this Indian, with two others, stopped near the ruins and called me to him. He leaned forward and whispered, "I am Paul; don't you know me? You must go with me to my tepee." I knew Paul very well at Yellow Medicine, as he was a farmer Indian; but he was disguised in his Indian costume, so I did not recognize him again. He was very anxious I should ride, but I dared not attempt to ride thirty miles on a mule bare-backed, when I never rode a horse with a saddle. My little boy knew him very well and was very anxious to go with him. I said to the child, "You will cry when night comes for me, because I shall walk, and not get to Yellow Medicine in two days." "No, no, mamma, I will not cry; I will die to walk so far; do let me go with Paul." I asked Chaska, who had just come up, if I had better try to go with Paul. He talked with Paul a few minutes, and then said I could go if I wished to, but that Paul wanted me for a wife, and had been for several days trying to get a white woman. He also said that Paul had told him that my husband was alive; they had all made their escape at the Agency the morning after I left. What glorious news was that for a wife who had mourned her husband as dead. I laughed, cried, and acted like a wild person. I could have danced with joy; my body as well as my mind felt lightened. I felt now as if I must live and try to save my children. A new impulse was given me from that hour. I told James he might go with Paul, for Chaska advised me to let him go, as our load was so large he could not ride. He said as he started, "I wish you would go, too, mamma," and seemed a little sorry I had consented to let him go. I now can see his little bare legs hanging down against the black ones of the Indian, and his white face looking so pitiful as he rode away. How many times that day I regretted that I let him leave me; sometimes I would think it might not be Paul and that I had been deceived, and probably I would never see him again. I saw him in all kinds of danger. I thought he might be sun struck, riding that extremely hot day without a shade for his little head. I was looking in all directions for his body. I suffered so much in my mind that I did not realize my bodily sufferings. The more I thought, the less hope I had of ever seeing him again; but then I thought that God could shield him from danger as well away from me as with me, and uttering a prayer in his behalf, I felt more calm and quiet, knowing he was in God's care.

I wish it was within my power to describe that procession as it moved over the prairie. I think it was five miles in length and one mile wide; the teams were very close together, and of every kind of vehicle that was ever manufactured. Nice coaches filled with young Indians, all dressed up in all kinds of finery, the more ridiculous the better they were pleased. White summer bonnets were considered great ornaments, but they were worn by men altogether. White crape shawls were wound around their black heads; gold watches tied around their ankles, the watches clattering as they rode. The squaws were dressed in silk short gowns, with earrings and breast-pins taken from the whites. It made my heart ache to see all this; still I could not keep from smiling at times to see how ridiculously they were used by these poor savage creatures; they looked indeed more like a troop of monkeys than anything human. Ox carts, chaises, buggies, baker's carts, peddler's wagons, all well filled with these creatures. Occasionally you would see the face of the white children intermixed with the Indian children. Sometimes you would see a cow with poles tied to her back, Indian style, and such a rearing, tearing and plunging was never seen before. It was ludicrous in the extreme, and many times I laughed until I could scarcely stand; for very often in their plunging they would upset some squaw, who had all her possessions on her back and out would roll a baby, a dog, bread, sugar, and sometimes flour, all mixed together, with a great deal of her wardrobe.

I saw a very nice buggy, with an Indian pony attached, that never felt a harness before, and such antics never was witnessed; everything was ornamented with green boughs, horses, men, women and children. United States flags were numerous, and many times it looked like "Uncle Sam's" camp. The noise of that train was deafening; mules braying, cows (poor animals) lowing, horses neighing, dogs barking and yelping as they were run over or trodden upon, children crying, kittens running, for a squaw always takes her pets with her; and then to increase the confusion, was musical instruments played by not very scientific performers, accompanied with the Indians singing the ever-lasting "Hi! Hi!" All these noises, together with the racket made by Little Crow's soldiers who tried, but in vain, to keep things in order, was like the confusion of Babel.

I traveled in great distress barefoot, trotting along in the tall, dry, prairie grass. In some places it was five feet high. My feet and legs were cut by the grass switching and twirling around them as we drove through regardless of how many prairie snakes we trod upon. I was obliged to keep up with the other *squaws,* and they will trot as fast as a horse.

At noon we stopped for dinner, which consisted of crackers, maple sugar and good cool water. Chaska, when seeing my feet, said I must ride, for the skin was all off from one foot, and both were running with blood. His mother washed them and, cleaned up some roots and wrapped them up; and when we started I was provided with a seat on the load and drove the horses the rest of the day. With what feelings I passed poor Gleason's body, no one knows. He was stripped of his clothing, except his shirt and drawers; his head had been crushed in by a stone. Now I was on this road going towards my once happy home, now desolate and destroyed; and he who I was last with on that road was lying there dead, to be gazed at and stoned by these savages. I could not help rejoicing that my bones were not there also. How I wished for power to punish Hapa on that spot, although I must say he never looked towards the remains of his victim; perhaps his conscience smote him for what he had done.

We did not travel many miles after dinner, as the report reached us that we were pursued by the white soldiers. What a scattering there was. All order was gone. All made for a little thicket, for nearly everyone knows that is the Indians' battle ground. Here were made preparations for a fight. Guns were discharged and reloaded; bullets were made; powder flasks were filled, and every man that night was ready for action. We camped two miles away from water, and I thought I would perish with thirst, but soon Chaska came in, bringing a large bag of thorns, *(sic)* which refreshed me. What thoughts passed through my mind as I sat there under the trees with these people. My husband I knew not where he was. My boy gone I knew not whither, as I still had doubts of Paul. I felt sometimes as if I would be carried to Yellow Medicine and then be murdered in sight of my home. I felt sure Chaska's family would protect me as long as they could, but every day we heard reports respecting the future disposal of us prisoners.

The Indians did not put up many tepees that night; nearly all slept in or under their wagons, to guard their horses or goods, for they were in constant fear of some evil—sometimes Chippewas, Sissetons, or white men. They did not enjoy their plunder very much nor very long. We started very early for Yellow Medicine. Soon we came in sight of Major Brown's house. Where now was all this family with their elegance and comforts? in an Indian's tepee, their home destroyed and their goods scattered! As we went farther on I could see our houses at the Agency. They looked just as they did when we left, as the buildings were not burned until Little Crow's soldiers came up; for they were in fear the soldiers would come up and occupy them as forts—they being all of brick. What a loss there was to the country by Sibley not hurrying on his forces, for all our furniture remained good for the three weeks after the people fled.

When we got to the top of the hill I had to get out and walk, as the hill was very steep. We crossed the Yellow Medicine river.

How differently everything looked from what it did only one week before. All the wooden buildings belonging to the traders, which were in the valley of the Yellow Medicine, were burned.

Soon we were obliged to rise the hill on the opposite side as the Agency is situated on a hill six hundred feet above the river; it was just at noon, the sun pouring down upon my head until I was nearly mad with headache and excitement, for I lost the old woman, and Winona would not wait for me, and I had to run to keep up with her as she would say, "You stop, the Indian soldiers will kill you." After rising the hill we walked two miles before we stopped. It was several hours before they could decide where to stop, and then we were without shade or a drop of water. I had not seen or heard anything of my boy; if I could have had him with me I could have borne all other trouble patiently.

About this time the old woman came, and some trouble arose between her and Winona about some shot that was lost, Winona accusing the old woman of stealing them; they were very abusive and at last Winona threw a tin kettle at the old woman, and she left, saying she would not stay any longer with her. When Chaska came I told him, and he said he should leave; that Hapa was all the time threatening me and my children because they ate so much. He said, "You go to my grandfather's; my mother is there and I will soon come." I went to their piece of ground, for they were not going to put up their tepees that night, so I was doomed to pass another night under a wagon. As for sleep, all I got was in the day time, for I was too nervous to sleep in the night.

Next morning after our arrival at Yellow Medicine, the Indian soldiers were determined the encampment should be in a circle, and the old woman got scared and hid me again for several hours. I could not find any one who knew where Paul was. I did not know his Indian name, and they did not know him by the name of Paul. Chaska said if my boy was not brought that night he would go to Hardwood the next morning for him, as that was where Paul formerly lived. My feet at this time were very bad; proud flesh as large as a silver dollar was eating into my foot, and the old woman said I must not walk any more for several days. Soon after she brought me out of my hiding place; she carried me to the camp. Everything was now still. She took me to her sister's tepee, who was a widow, the same person that I had stayed one night with at Redwood. She prepared me a good breakfast of coffee, fried meat, and potatoes and fried bread, but I could not eat, my mind was so troubled about my child. While I was sitting on the ground, drinking my coffee, a lady appeared before me whom I had known at Redwood and also at Shakopee, but had not seen her since I was in captivity before. She was feeling very badly, and complained much of her treatment, saying she had no place decent to sleep, or anything fit for a pig to eat, and begged what I had for herself and children. I pitied her very much, for many nights she said she and her children were driven out of the tepee while the medicine men were at work over a wounded man who was with them.

That afternoon, just as I had got my feet done up nicely, and Chaska had started after my boy, some one said the Indians were becoming drunk. I did not feel alarmed until Chaska drove up to

the tepee very much excited; his horse was just dripping with perspiration, as if he had been out in the rain, and he said a white
woman had just been killed not far from us by a drunken man, and
that I must hide somewhere. An old squaw I had known at Yellow
Medicine, called "Aga," was just in to see me, and she said she
would take me up to the friendly camp of Yellow Medicine
Indians, who were always encamped about one mile from us. She
took Nellie on her back and we ran for some cornfields, stooping
down so we could not be seen, around through the potato fields
until we got out of sight of the lower camp, and at last arrived at
the tepee, torn, worn, and nearly exhausted. No one knows unless
they have run for their life, how a person feels, expecting every
moment to be overtaken; and when they reach a place of safety
how relieved they feel. When I got to Bit-Nore's tepee, the name
of her husband, I felt so happy that I dropped upon my knees and
thanked God that he had once more brought me away from death.

I felt that night very happy, as a young half-breed girl told me
she had seen James that day, and he was well and happy, and the
old Bit-Nore prepared something for my feet that eased the pain
very much. Bit-Nore was Chaska's cousin, and he was a very good
man. He was a farmer at Yellow Medicine, and one of my nearest
neighbors. I don't wish any one to think he was Cut-Nore, for that
wretch was hanged, while Bit-Nore was taken care of and protected all winter by the government and now has gone to
Missouri.

The morning following my arrival at Bit-Nore's tepee, Chaska
drove up in a buggy and had my child with him. I did not at first

recognize him, his dress was so different from when I saw him last.

As I went towards him, saying, "My child, my son," he was busy showing some plaything to the Indian children collected around; the little rogue manifested no joy at seeing me. I said, "James, ain't you glad to see your mother?" "Oh, yes, but then I had such a nice time at Paul's, I want to go back again." I tried to take him from the buggy and he said, "Do you think I am a baby, I can get out alone now." I thought he was getting very old, for he was not five until October. This night I was happy. I had my children both in my arms, and I thought I never will murmur again if I can only keep them with me. I knew my husband was alive, and I was out of reach of that villain, Hapa's, clutches. I sang for the children, that night; we ran around on the prairie, picked flowers, and my spirits were as light as air, although I was still a prisoner. Do you who may read this think I did wrong? Many persons say I was happy with the Indians, that I did not mourn over my lot as many. Why should I mourn all the time, could I effect any good by so doing? No; instead of good I should have made trouble for myself. I tried to make myself as pleasant as I could while I was with my Indian friends, and in that way they learned to respect me more every day.

I felt the change from civilized to savage life as much as any one, but it would do no good to keep drawing comparisons. I was there, and it was no use to try to borrow trouble, but try to be as contented as I could under the circumstances, but every word and action has been remembered, and turned against me to my disadvantage.

After remaining at this camp two days, Aga said I had better return, for Paul was determined to have me for his wife, and if I went back to Chaska's tepee I would be more safe than with them. She sent for him to come, but as it drew near night, and he came not, she took Nellie and we started back. We met him, and we all got in and rode back in his aunt's. James was much disturbed to think he should be out that day, as it was raining, for he was very well dressed in his new Indian costume, made for him by Paul's wife, and he was afraid of his soiling it. I went to Chaska's aunt's, and he said I must stay there until his mother made her a tepee, and I must help her. Chaska had lived in a house previous to the outbreak, was a good farmer, and worked hard. When forced to leave his house he was obliged to go with his sister and her husband, as they had no tepee. His wife had been dead but a few months and he was still wearing mourning for her. I remained with his aunt, assisting his mother to make our tepee, sitting out in the hot sun sewing, the white cloth drawing more heat towards us. I was afraid my eyes would be injured, but I see no change in my person only the color. I do not think I will ever recover from the sunburn.

Just before the battle of Birch Coolie, Chaska said he was going to the Big Woods to drive up cattle, and I had better go back to Bit-Nore's again, and said his mother would go with me.

I saw the lady I spoke of again this day; her tepee was near ours. She was very unhappy, and begged me to ask her people to give her a squaw dress, as I could speak Dakota. She was very filthy, and so were her children. I think she suffered very much more in that way than any other prisoner. She often said she envied me, I was so comfortably situated. The night before I went to Bit-Nore's the last time, she said she was going to a half-breed's, and I did not see her again, as she made her escape. We all thought she was murdered, for the Indians had learned to dislike her very much, as she was constantly fretting about her situation, and saying what she would like to do with the Indians. It was poor policy on her part, for if she had not been taken away privately to the friendly Indians, her life would have been sacrificed by Little Crow's soldiers.

I went to Bit-Nore's again, but I cannot remember how long I stayed there, but it was after the battle of Birch Coolie, for the next morning after that fight I removed with their family farther up the country with sad feelings. I gazed on my home, as it was enveloped in flames the morning we started. I had very little hopes of ever seeing that place again, for the Indians said that they were going to the Red River now without stopping again, and I thought I should surely die before reaching there. Chaska had always said the soldiers would soon come and you will be rescued; and he promised me if they came not before the river began to freeze, he would try to take me down in a canoe; but said I had better wait for the soldiers, for if we were discovered by the Indians we would all be killed. I tried to keep up good courage, but it was with a sad heart I drove myself and children over that prairie that day. I have driven many horses, but none compared with the one I drove that day. He was an Indian pony, and I should judge had a good deal of mule about him, for he would go just contrary to the lines. I was amused but at the same time I was vexed, and I often thought of the picture we made. I was kept constantly busy trying to keep things straight; the back part of our wagon was piled high above our heads with goods, and under our feet; and the seat of the wagon was what had been our pantry. My feet were astride a jar of lard, melted like oil; a crock of molasses, a pan with flour, with bread, vegetables, dishes, all mixed up together. Now it was quite an undertaking to keep all things in order—pony, two children, and party.

We got along very well, considering all things, until I got to a creek, when the pony, not having had water that morning, became much excited for a drink, and plunged forward regardless of his precious freight; but he did not go far, for he was soon fast in the mud. I unloaded my passengers with help, and gave a jump, thinking I should reach a nice piece of grass; but when I struck I was fast to my knees in a patch of boggy ground. How I was to extricate myself I knew not; but I laughed at the thought of my predicament. At last the children began calling, "Mamma, what are you doing down in the mud?" I found I could not get out without help, and called to Bit-Nore's girl to come to my assistance. She brought a board and I got out; but what a sight I was! completely covered with mud in my struggles to free myself.

Pony, as soon as released of his load, rushed into the water, got a drink, hurried himself up the bank, regardless of our provisions. My blanket was considerably soiled, but everything was otherwise safe. We rode the rest of the way quietly, but my boy would occasionally say, "Mamma, why don't you turn round and drive to Shakopee?" I said, "Why, you know the Indians would not let us."

"Oh, dear me! mamma, what do you suppose God made Indians for? I wish they were all dead, don't you, mamma?"

We camped about three miles west of Hazelwood, but it was a long time, as usual, before they could decide upon the best place. This day I was treated with bread and molasses; the children thinking it a treat, as we sat eating it, under the wagon, on a piece of carpet which they always provided me with. I heard a voice in my own language, and Miss E. B – – came towards me. Glad was I to see her. I knew she was a prisoner, but had not caught a glimpse of her since I had been in captivity. She looked finely in her squaw dress, but did not compliment me very highly on my looks. She said she would not have known me if she had met me on the prairie, for I was so much changed. My hair turned as white as an old woman's with fright the night I was taken prisoner.

After being at Bit-Nore's some days, I got nervous, and wished to go to the old woman's for the Yellow Medicine Indians were expected to be attacked every night by the Lower Indians, because they would not come and join them in their camp.

Aga said she would like me to stay, but told me I would be more safe if I was back with Chaska, so they sent for him. He disliked to have me leave Bit-Nore's, because if we traveled I could ride, if I was with them, and if with him I must walk, as they had but one horse now. He and Hapa had separated, but all I thought of was life. I preferred to go back even if I had to walk, rather than stay, expecting death every minute as I did. Chaska and his cousin, Dowonca, came for me; one took Nellie, the other James on their horses, and I followed by their side.

Little Crow's camp had not crossed the creek, therefore it was three miles from the Yellow Medicine camp. When we were going along I could see Mr. Riggs' church and house all in flames.

I think I suffered in my mind more at Yellow Medicine and that neighborhood, than at any other spot, as it recalled so many pleasant scenes past and gone; it spoke so forcibly of home, husband, children, all united; now where were we, and what would be our fate? Would we ever be together again?

I got back to Chaska's tepee, and it seemed good to get back, for everything was so clean, new and sweet. I was nearly devoured with fleas at Bit-Nore's, for they had thirteen dogs. About this time my boy became quite sick, and I thought for many days he would die. I was told that in Dr. Williamson's house, which was as yet unburnt, I could find medicine. I asked Chaska to take me there, as it was several miles, and I dared not go alone. One day he took James and me and his cousin, and we visited the house, where I often went while at home. What a change! Their once happy home was all destroyed. It looked as if an earthquake had done its worst work, for everything was broken up and mixed together. Bedsteads, stoves, books, and medicines. I could not keep from shrinking as I thought of the old people, that had passed all their lives among these same people, and now how they were repaid!

The bell from the top of the building was being rung furiously by some boys; the Indians were tearing, crushing everything within their reach. I went into the garden and gathered a few tomatoes, and came away feeling very, very sad.

While at this camp I suffered very much bringing water, as the bank was almost perpendicular; all the way I could get up would be by catching a twig with one hand, and pull myself up, and then catch another. Many times the twig would break, and down I would go, feet foremost, to the bottom, deluged by the water I was carrying.

One day I went for water, and as my feet were dirty, I thought I would wash them; as the pail was an old one I thought I would wash my feet in it, for I could reach the water only by lying down on my face; so I thought I would dip it up and wash, and then wash the pail. When I got back to the tepee the family were all in a great commotion. Chaska brought in an interpreter, who said I had committed a great sin by putting my feet in the pail, for all vessels belonging to a tepee are sacred, and no women are allowed to put their feet in them or step over them. I told him I would scrub the pail, but he said it would not do, for they would never use it again, and they did not. It was turned upside down, and when we removed, they left it on the prairie. Speaking of their superstitions, reminds me of many things that were interesting to me, and I will relate them here. Their war spears and medicine bags are sacred things; a female is never allowed to touch them.

By day they are tied to a pole in front of the tepee; at night they are brought in and tied high above the head of the chief man in the tepee. One morning I noticed they were about to fall down and was going to fasten them up, when the old woman said, "Stop, stop, white woman, stop, I will call some man." She appeared much frightened, and run in a great hurry and brought a boy. When the men go to battle they always take their spears with them, thinking a few painted sticks will assist them in their under-taking.

I offended many an Indian God by stepping over axes, pipes, or persons feet, or some such silly thing. They never wash their hands in any dish, they fill their mouths and then spit it out on their hands. I could not do this way, so they begged me a wash dish from some half-breeds.

I don't remember what time in the month we started for Red Iron's village, but I have not forgotten what I suffered that day, for I had to walk all the distance, which was sixteen miles. My mare that Chaska had, was this day, for the first time, hitched to poles, Indian fashion. Poor animal, I felt bad for her as she had been made a great pet of by myself and husband. When the poles were fastened on and she took a few steps, she began prancing, which threw everything in all directions. As soon as she got quiet they put James on her back, and with Nellie on mine, the old woman leading the horse, we commenced our march towards Lac Que Parle; we walked without resting even for a drink of water, sixteen miles. They seemed to feel very bad because they could not give me a ride, but it was no use to mourn, every one had a load without taking me, and so I plodded on, sometimes as Nellie would fall asleep the old woman would tie her on to the bundle, which was fastened to the poles, and she would ride until a sudden jolt would awaken her, then I would have to quiet her and would be forced to walk as fast as the horse to keep her quiet. The sun is very powerful on these prairies, and the dust was stifling, and the perspiration and the dust did not add to my looks. I would hear the

Indians say, "White woman got a dirty face," but had no idea how I looked until I went to the river (my looking glass) to arrange my dress. The last few miles we traveled that day I experienced more pain than I ever did in my life before. I might have been tracked by the blood that ran from my feet and legs, cut by the tall dry grass; we could not go in the road, but right on the prairie, the carriages filling the road. Glad was I when we made a stop, and I told Chaska that I would certainly die if I had to walk any farther. He said he was sorry, but he wanted me to stay at Bit-Nore's so I could ride, but I would not, and all he could do for me he had done, and he said I had better go back now, but I preferred to remain with his family to going back and being killed by Little Crow.

We remained at Red Iron's village some little time. While there letters were carried to Fort Ridgely, from Little Crow to H.H. Sibley. One morning Tom Robertson and another man, a half-breed, went with letters; soon after the Indian soldiers left, crossed the river, and all in our neighborhood believed they had gone to intercept and murder them. There was great alarm, for the Indians said if they killed them they would return and kill all the rest of the half-breeds and prisoners. When I heard this I dropped as one struck with apoplexy; I could not speak for awhile, my teeth chattered and I shivered with fear. I then thought of what Chaska had many times told me, that if I was in danger, to tell the Indians I was his wife, and I would be saved. So I said to an Indian, "I am Chaska's wife, will they kill me?" He said, "No," but he believed I was telling an untruth. I went back to the old woman's and told Chaska. He said I had done very wrong in saying so, for there was no truth in the story. He was quite angry with me for saying so. But I did not consider how it would sound. I would have called myself the evil spirit's wife if I thought by so doing I could save my life. I suppose many Indians really thought I was his wife, for there was such an excitement all the time I forgot all about contradicting it. One day before this a half-breed woman came in and a white woman was with her. They said that Little Crow was going to destroy all the whites, but would spare all that had Indian blood in them. I made up this story, which I will relate here. I said I was safe, as I was part Indian. I knew the lady had known me in Shakopee many years, and she said she did not believe me. I said I was an eighth-breed; that my grandfather married a squaw many years ago in the West, and took her East, and I was one of her descendents; that I had some pride about acknowledging it, but now perhaps it would save my life. I then asked her if she did not remember how very dark my mother was; when she became convinced. I was sure this half-breed woman would tell it all around, and I would be spared. I knew it was wrong to tell such falsehoods, but I felt as if my God knew my thoughts, and he would pardon me for doing as I did. Now to this day that woman believes me part Indian, because I never had an opportunity to contradict it.

While we were camped at Mare Shoe, or Red Iron's, the camp was very quiet; soldiers would go off in scouting parties, but the majority of the Indians were around playing cards, shooting at ducks, &c. The old women were busy drying corn and potatoes, cutting and drying beef, laying in a stock for winter. I assisted at all these operations willingly, for I thought they might save my children from starvation on those plains, where we were bound, for I have given up all hopes of being rescued by Sibley. I had not many idle moments. I made short gowns for the squaws, made bread, fried meat and potatoes, brought water, and went to the river three or four times every day to wash my baby's clothing, for her diarrhea was growing worse daily. It was quite amusing to see us white women at the river washing. The banks for several miles usually were lined with Indians with their horses and cattle, boys and squaws swimming, causing it to be very muddy, so we would go out up to our waists to get a clear drink or a place to wash. When we finished we would come out and shake ourselves like dogs and go back to our tepees with our wet bundles on our backs. I have slept many a night in my wet clothes, and never took a cold while I was there.

The Indians were all very kind to me, they brought me books and papers to read, and I would make them shirts, so as to return their favors. Many times when I have been coming up the steep banks of the river, all out of breath, bringing water, some Indian would take my pails out of my hands and carry them for me. Now this for a white man would not be considered much, but for an Indian it is a great thing, for they never bring wood or water. Every little act like that I remember, and let who blame me that I shall say there are many, very good, kind hearted Indians. In the nights, while we were at Red Iron's we had a good chance to sleep, for the young men had great dances and councils, so it left the old women and myself time to rest. Before that time hardly a night passed without our cooking all night, as they would have a tepee full of company playing cards and singing.

After leaving Red Iron village there was no rest, either night or day, for they knew when the soldiers left the Fort, and they expected they would come right on. Many a time I have run for the woods with the squaws, thinking the soldiers were very near, and they said Sibley was going to fire shells into the camp.

Every night now, the old woman kept watch, keeping the door open so as to watch their horses, for we were drawing near the Sisseton country, and Standing Buffalo had threatened to take all their horses and cattle, if they came up where he was.

I should have suffered with the cold at this time if Chaska and his mother had not been so kind as to lend me their blankets to cover me, and they would draw around the fire to keep warm. Where could you find white people that would do like that? Go without to cover others? Was this kindness or not, let me ask you?

The Indians made much sport of the slow movements of Sibley; said the white people did not care much about their wives and children, or they would have hurried on faster.

Many nights the old crier would go around, saying that the soldiers are coming, make ready for battle. Sometimes he would say, the white women are to be killed in the morning; and our feelings were dreadful living in that way. Then when morning came they would tell a different story. Little Crow had a plan like this: when the soldiers came he was going to send us out in our squaw dress, therefore causing the white men to kill those they came to rescue. I had no fears of anything of this kind. When Standing

Buffalo came, Chaska was very nervous. The lower Indians were very much afraid of the Sissetons, and they thought he would say kill the white women, but he came and shook hands with some of us, and said, that if the Indians brought us up into his country he would take us and bring us back to our friends.

When the news came that Sibley was near Yellow Medicine, and that the Indians were going down to fight him, I felt very uneasy, for Chaska said he and his cousins were going, and I would be left without any protection. He and many others went, and I passed a wretched day. We heard all kinds of reports about the friendly Indian camp, that Little Crow had threatened before leaving. About nine o'clock in the evening Chaska returned, saying that Little Crow was a bad man, and he would not go again unless he was forced to. He remained at home two days, when it seemed as if the squaws were crazy; they would move their tepees every few hours, sometimes on the prairie, then into the timber.

One morning a messenger came, saying that every man that could carry a gun should come down immediately, or he would shoot all that refused. I tried to urge Chaska not to go, but he said Little Crow would say I had prevented him, and that he would destroy us both. The morning he left he seemed very anxious to impress upon my mind the necessity of remaining with his mother. Several times he came in and said, "You stay where you are; don't go up to the friendly camp; don't you talk to any half-breed or white women, if you do you will be killed." I knew these Indians were trying to get the prisoners, now that they knew Sibley was coming, and I thought he was fearful I would go off, as some had done. After he had been gone sometime, his cousin, a half-breed, told me that Little Crow intended to destroy the friendly camp as soon as he returned; therefore Chaska's anxiety to have me stay where I was.

I stayed with his mother as I promised, although all left but two other Americans besides myself. If Little Crow had been victorious, all would have been killed; but God ordered otherwise, and they were all saved.

Chaska was gone two days and one night. When he returned, I inquired how the battle had gone; he said they had killed one hundred and fifty white men, and only lost two Indians. I felt as if all hope was now gone, and could not help saying that I believed the Lord was on their side. But night told different stories, and I should have known it from the mourning and crying from many tepees, if they had not told me. Any one that has heard one squaw lament can judge the noise of four or five hundred all crying at once. As soon as it was dark, Chaska advised me to lie down so my shadow would not show on the tepee cloth, as he was afraid they might shoot through and kill me, they were so excited. They had a council that night, and they decided to give us up, and I was told that a letter would be sent to Sibley the next morning, requesting him to come for us in the morning. They had many plans. They did not get breakfast—only some roasted potatoes in the ashes, and commenced packing up, preparing for a start. I asked if they were not going to give us up; they said some were, but others were going to take their prisoners with them. I asked how or where we would be given up; they said five half-breeds would take us down to Sibley's camp. I then said I would not go, for I knew we would all be killed by Little Crow's soldiers. I told them I had rather remain with them and wait until Sibley came. Soon the camp began to break up, and the old woman gave me some potatoes, saying that I must eat them, as upon the plains where we were going, we could get more. I threw myself down, crying, on the ground. Chaska said, "What are you crying about?" I said, "I did not wish to go away with the Indians." He said, "You did not wish to go with the half-breeds; what will you do? The Indians are all going very soon." I told him I thought the Indians were going to wait for Sibley, and try to make peace. He said they were afraid to stay for fear they would all be killed, and were going on, leaving us with the half-breeds. Soon after this conversation, two chiefs came in, saying "Joe Campbell was going for Other Day," the Indian who rescued the people from death at Yellow Medicine. In the meantime they wished me to write an account of my treatment by Chaska, and the other Indians I had been acquainted with. I told them it was very foolish for me to write, for I could tell the people just as well as to write, and I began to be suspicious of some evil. I was afraid they would murder us and hide our bodies, and carry our notes to the Fort. I wrote the note, but was determined I would not go without more protection than five men over that prairie.

Soon after writing the note, I was told to hurry and change my dress for one of my own, for the soldiers were coming, and it would be wrong for them to see me in a squaw dress. I dressed in a great hurry. I could not tell what was to be done, there were so many stories. At last we were ready, and we left our tepee and my Indian friends, who had given me a home and protected me for six weeks. The old woman shook hands and kissed me, and said, "You are going back where you will have good, warm houses and plenty to eat, and we will starve on the plains this winter. Oh! that 'bad man,' who has caused so much trouble, meaning Little Crow. They cried over James, and begged me to leave him with them. He was a great favorite with the Indians all the time I was with them. Chaska led Mr. Gleason's dog. Dowonca carried James, and I with Nellie, we started for the Indian soldiers' camp. A large American flag was flying, and we sat ourselves down on the grass beneath its folds, awaiting the decision of our captors relative to our going or staying. All seemed anxious to have us go, still none wished to go below, but a few half-breeds. At last they said they would carry us down; then I began to act like one crazy. I declared I would not go; whereupon Mr. Campbell said I could go and stay with his wife, who was a white woman, until his return, as the friendly Indians were going to stay where they were. We stayed on this hill until Little Crow's camp had gone, then we went over to the friendly camp, Chaska and his mother bidding me good-bye, and leaving.

I went to Mrs. R – – 's tepee; her husband is a half-breed. She was like a wild woman. She was afraid to speak, fearing she might be heard by Indian spies. There were about sixty tepees left in the morning after the others had gone. Instead of taking us below, the Indians left us and went on horseback, carrying letters to Sibley, hurrying him on—telling him how we were situated—that we were liable to be attacked any moment by Little Crow's soldiers. I had not been in Mrs. R – – 's tepee more than an hour, when her husband came in saying many Indians were returning, and were anxious to camp with us; among them was Chaska and all his family. Soon Eagle Head appeared, and said I had better come back to Chaska's tepee; that they had decided to remain, and would feel more safe if I was with them when Sibley came. He also said if Little Crow returned, as they expected he would at night I would be more safe with them than with the half-breeds; so I decided to go, as his tepee was not more than three rods from Mrs. R – – 's. She was quite angry because I left, said I must be crazy, for he would kill me. I told her they had protected me for six weeks, and I was not afraid of their injuring me now. But I knew her object in having me stay, for she said that Wara-cota-mong had no prisoner to give up to Sibley, and she wished me to go to his tepee, so he could have the credit of releasing me. I felt if I could be of any service to any one, I would rather benefit those that had taken care of me when I was in danger, than to favor strange Indians. I many times sent for this lady, when I was a prisoner, but she dared not come; so she knew not of their kindness to me.

Among those who decided to remain were Wabasha, Wacota, and parts of several bands.

The half-breeds returned from Sibley's camp early in the afternoon. We looked for the soldiers all night, but they came not. There was no sleep. Every man was on guard. Intrenchments were dug around our tepees, and pits within, for we expected we would be attacked before morning, for Little Crow's brother had remained around as a spy, and surely would notify Little Crow of the nonappearance of our soldiers.

We passed a very anxious night. Morning came, but no soldiers were visible. "What can be the matter?" was the cry. Some Indians came in, saying they had returned because their force was not large enough. Chaska became frightened, and said he thought I had better go to some half-breeds, and take his mother with me, and he would go off. Miss E. B – – and I persuaded him to remain, promising him our protection. He said he felt as if they would kill all the Indians; but we told him if Sibley had promised to shake hands with all that remained and gave up their prisoners, he would do as he said. At last he decided to stay, saying, "If I am killed, I will blame you for it." Now I will always feel that I am responsible for that man's murder, and I will never know quietness again.

How we looked for Sibley all the next day, but he did not come; all that night we watched also, but no signs of him yet. Where can he be? he was only twenty-five miles away. We at last concluded he was afraid. The Indians began to get uneasy, and said "Little Crow will be back and kill us all, if Sibley does not come soon." How we blamed him for making us suffer as we did, for we expected death every instant. The second night we waited for him, an Indian came in saying they had only traveled eight miles, and it was now thirty-six hours since he got our message, and they had camped for the night, spending hours to intrench themselves. An army of over two thousand leaving us, a little handful of persons, with only about one hundred men to protect us! The time taken to intrench themselves, passed in marching, would have brought them to our relief, but God watched over us, and kept those savages back. To Him I give all the honor and glory; Sibley I do not even thank, for he deserved it not.

The second night of our stay, Dowonca had a religious performance in our tepee. The females were excluded. They were trying to ascertain by their conjuring if the soldiers would hurt them.

That night every Indian was on guard, the report reaching us that Little Crow was advancing towards us for battle.

There were no more midnight councils and dances; all was still and quiet, except the medicine men at their performances over the sick. The Indians believe when a person is sick they are possessed with evil spirits; and when these conjurers stand over them and rattle gourds, thinking by so doing they will drive out the evil spirits; and when some are about leaving, the squaws rush at the imaginary beings and pretend to shoot them, or stab them with their knives, all the time singing, talking, imploring their gods to help them. It is enough to make a well person sick. I was one day in a tepee where an Indian woman was in labor; she had been suffering many hours, and these conjurers were at work rattling and singing. Her husband soon came in and began cutting out little images of stained hide. I was told that he would stand at the door of the tepee, and, as occasion required, throw one at her, expecting this would assist nature in bringing forth the child.

Poor superstitious beings, how much they are to be pitied! Very few of them believe in any God besides a painted stone or stick; ought we to expect these creatures to act with reason and judgement like ourselves?

Just for one moment, think of all they have borne for years, and you will wonder, as I do, that they saved as many lives as they did, for their religion teaches them that evil for evil, good for good, is right. Many asked me why they killed so many that had befriended them. I myself asked that question many times while I was with them, and I will give one answer that was given me.

An Indian, having plenty of ducks, went one day to Beaver Creek, and wished to exchange them for potatoes. He said, when telling me of it, that his ducks were fresh and good; that they took them and gave him potatoes that a hog could not eat, they were so soft. Now this is the way many befriended the Indians: gave them what they could not eat themselves. This is the way the Indians have been treated for years. I know the Indians have butchered the whites, and I wish every guilty one punished; but I cannot blame them as many do, for I am sure they had cause, and very strong reasons for being revenged on some of the persons who had been living off their lands and money, while they were starving. If these Indians had commenced this outbreak out of pure wickedness, I would feel as many do: that they ought to be exterminated; but it is not so; they took the only way they knew of getting restitution, and we all want that if we are wronged.

I have many very firm friends in the Indian camp, and I feel for them as much pity and sorrow as if they were white; for I have sat and listened to their tales of suffering and distress, until my heart bled for them, I pray God they may for the future be more mercifully dealt with by those that are in authority over them.

To return to my narrative: the night passed without an attack, as was anticipated; but we could hear no tidings of the soldiers, and we really thought they had returned. Sibley had requested us to remain where we were, or we should have gone down. That was the message brought back by the half-breeds. Now it was the third day, and we were getting very impatient, but not as much so as our Indian friends, who very often said, "We will go on; there is no use waiting longer." About noon of the third day we saw them coming, and then, instead of joy, I felt feelings of anger enter my breast, as I saw such an army, for I felt that part at least might have come to our rescue before that late hour. While they were coming up we saw a party very near us, and several half-breeds and Indians started for them, and found them to be a party of Sissetons who had come up just in advance of the soldiers, bringing with them three prisoners—one girl and two boys. Joe Campbell demanded the children, but they refused to give them up, and said they were going to kill them; but Joe made a sudden spring and secured one, while the Indians saved the boys, when the Sissetons fled. I conversed with the girl; she said they were near the soldiers for a long time, so she could hear their voices; that they crawled on their knees much of the time, to avoid being seen. Her feet were all blisters, but the boys the Indians carried part of the way. It seems very strange they should spare so many helpless children, and murder their parents, when they are such a trouble to them; for I have seen squaws carry white children nine and ten years old on their backs, and let their own walk. Now this was out of real good feeling, for they certainly had no selfish motives in so doing, and the world does the Indian great injustice when they say they saved persons only for selfish purposes.

As Sibley's forces drew near, the Indians became much

alarmed, and drew within their tepees. We were all eager to go to them immediately, but were told we should remain where we were until Sibley came over.

The soldiers encamped about a quarter of a mile from our camp. Sibley sent a messenger, saying, that he would come over after dinner and talk with the Indians.

My dinner was eaten for the last time with my Indian friends; they were very sad; seemed to be dreading some evil. About three o'clock Sibley and staff arrived, and after conversing a few minutes with the Indians, ordered those having prisoners to bring them forward, and give them up. Old Eagle Head and Chaska came for me; before leaving the old woman tore her shawl and gave me half, as I had none.

Chaska trembled with fear. He said, "You are a good woman, you must talk good to your white people, or they will kill me; you know I am a good man, and did not shoot Mr. Gleason, and I saved your life. If I had been a bad man I would have gone with those bad chiefs." I assured him he need not fear, they would not injure him; but how vain were all my promises; poor man, he found the white deceitful, even unto his death.

After I was introduced to Sibley, Mr. Riggs, and others, they requested me to point out the Indian who had saved me. He came forward as I called his name; and when I told them how kind he had been they shook hands with him, and made quite a hero of him, for a short time. I was compelled to leave the circle about this time, on account of my baby, and went to a tepee near, and while there the company broke up, taking the white women with them;

two or three of the officers remained to escort me over. When I got to the camp I found the soldiers in a state of great excitement, and all were eager to catch a glimpse of us. I was conducted to a large tent and soon it was surrounded with soldiers. We nearly suffocated for want of air. The tent I was in contained twenty-four persons. We suffered much for want of bedding, for there was no provision made for us, although they were so many weeks preparing for a start to rescue us. My children took very bad colds; I wished many times I had a tepee to sleep in. Now I wish to be distinctly understood in this remark; I did not wish myself back in a tepee, I only wanted the comforts of one; for I was a vast deal more comfortable with the Indians in every respect, than I was during my stay in that soldiers camp, and was treated more respectfully by those savages, than I was by those in that camp. We were given some straw to lie on, and a blanket for each. We must cook our own food exposed to the gaze of several hundred ignorant men, that would surround our fires as soon as we commenced cooking, so we could not breathe for want of air. I have many times been forced to go to some officer and request a guard around us, so we could cook without molestation. With the Indians my life was very different; the old squaws doing all the cooking, unless I took a fancy to assist.

The nights had got to be very cold now, and our tent was constructed for a stove, but we had none. Sometimes we would make a fire on the ground, and we would be forced to lie down on our faces, the smoke was so dense.

My clothing consisted of a thin gingham dress, one cotton

shirt, no under garments of any kind. I had a pair of moccasins, but no stockings, and half of a shawl. I am a large woman, and the squaws could not fix any that would be large enough. I weighed three days before the outbreak, two hundred and three pounds. When I got to Shakopee, eight weeks after, I weighed one hundred and sixty-three pounds. My travels and anxiety had worn upon me so much.

The first evening I passed at Camp Release was a very pleasant one. We were serenaded, and all the dainties of the camp were brought to us. I think the soldiers must have thought we had fasted for many weeks, to judge by the quantity brought to us. My children never knew what it was to be hungry, for food was plenty, and that which was good. Nearly every day some little dainty was brought to "Pojuta-Wacusta-Tanica"—English doctor's wife. I really thought my children would be made sick by the Indians, for they were continually feeding them.

I will here say, that the family I was with were not the greasy, lousy, filthy Indians, we used to see around begging. There is a great difference in them, and a person visiting the Agencies would have been astonished to see the hard working men and women, but clean and neat as our own farmers. I have employed squaws in my family that were educated by the missionaries, that could read and write in their own language, and could make coats, pants, or shirts, far better than many a white girl of the present generation. Such are some of the good works of the missionaries.

I always had in our tepee, a towel, soap, and wash dish; and I never knew any of the family to neglect washing and combing before eating. I had my own corner of the tepee, and was not allowed to go over to the other part, and they never came near mine.

They are foolishly particular about some things. The fire is in the centre of the tepee, and I was never allowed to pass around the fire. I must go out on my own side, for I would be going into my neighbors domains, if I went across. I used to get very tired sitting in one place with my baby. My little boy, however, enjoyed his life while there, for I could raise the tepee cloth and watch him; and he would play for hours on the grass, with the Indian boys.

I often asked him if he would not like to see his father, and he would answer, very indifferently, "Yes, but I wish he would come here, I would like to stay if he would."

The morning after my arrival at Camp Release I went over to the Indian's camp for some articles I left, in company with some ladies and gentlemen. We attended, while there, a Dakota prayer meeting. Chaska was much frightened; called me to the door, and said they had arrested two Indians, and if he was arrested he would know I had told falsehoods about him, and then he would lie, too.

I told him I had a long conversation with one of the officers, and he said that he should be pardoned on account of his kindness to me and my children. He appeared much pleased, and I went back to Camp Release. In the afternoon they had a sort of court of inquiry, and we were all questioned by Col. Crooks and Marshall, J.V.D. Hurd; S.R. Riggs, and others. I was the first one questioned. I related to them briefly what I have here written, after which Col. Marshall, said, "If you have anything more of a

private nature to relate, you can communicate it to Mr. Riggs." I
did not fully understand until he explained himself more fully. I
told them it was just as I related, it was all. They thought it very
strange that I had no complaints to make, but did not appear to
believe me. I was then told I might go, and not wishing to walk a
quarter of a mile alone, I went to a tepee near by occupied by Miss
La Flambois. While there, I sent for Chaska; he was looking very
pale and frightened. He said the white men were not doing as they
promised, and he knew they would kill him. I endeavored to persuade him to leave, promising him to take care of his mother. He
said, "No, I am not a coward, I am not afraid to die; all I care about
is my poor old mother, she will be left alone." He said he was sorry
I had persuaded him to remain; that his mother was very angry
with me for not letting him go. I still held out strong hopes to
him, insisting that he should be spared. Soon after I left he was
arrested; I was not much concerned at first, for I supposed he
would be soon liberated, unless they could find something more
against him than I knew of. That evening many officers were in,
laughing and talking; we were all acting like children let loose
from school, not really sensible of what we were saying, when
some one remarked, "We have seven of those Indians fast." When
Capt. Grant said, "Yes, we have seven of the black devils, and
before to-morrow night they will hang as high as Haman." I asked
if they had him who protected me. He said, "Yes, and he will
string with the rest." Then I made this remark, "Captain Grant, if
you hang that man I will shoot you, if it is not in twenty years."
Then thinking how it sounded, I said, "But first you must teach

me how to shoot, for I am afraid of a gun, unloaded even." Now this remark has been reported throughout the State. Any one well acquainted with me knows my violent impulsive disposition, and would not heed what I say when I am excited, for I very often say to my children, when I am out of patience, "Do be quiet, or I will whip you to death." Now I never meant to do one any more than I did the other; it is a rude way I have of expressing myself.

The first man tried was the negro, and several days were passed in bringing in testimony, when every one knew he was guilty. But it gave Little Crow a good chance to escape, therefore prolonging this war; for Little Crow was only six miles away when Sibley arrived. Now arises a thought, an inquiry: If Sibley had not found us waiting on that prairie for him, would he have returned, or would he have gone farther? If he intended to go farther, why did he stop where he did? for he was sure of the Indians, who had been waiting two days and nights for him. Why did he not push on and capture those murderers? Instead of so doing, the whole command stopped, and spent days and weeks trying men who had willingly given themselves up, leaving their chiefs and bands. I, as a woman, know very little about war; but I know Little Crow and his soldiers might have been captured last fall; but now it is very doubtful if he ever is overtaken. But I suppose the troops were fatigued, if they marched all the way from St. Paul as fast as they did from Yellow Medicine—taking over fifty hours to travel twenty-five miles.

I don't wish to censure those that were compelled to do as they were bidden, by their leaders. If those officers had known their wives and daughters were in danger, they would have found ways and means to travel more than five miles a day.

From the way the affair was conducted, I suppose if Sibley had not found us on the prairie, he would have returned, and we would have passed the winter on the plains; for he went no farther, as he said he could not pursue them without cavalry. He did, after a few weeks had passed, send out scouting parties, when he knew the Indians were returning to surrender. But he nor his troops never captured an Indian, (and I don't believe ever will, until there is a change made in our officers,) only those that wished to be taken, they preferring captivity to death by starvation. I never can give Sibley any credit in releasing the prisoners; but God influenced those Indians to remain with us, and to God and the Indians I give my thanks.

After I heard that Chaska was in prison, I was unhappy. I felt as if the Indians, as well as myself, had been deceived. All the solemn promises I had made to Chaska were as naught. What would he think of me? I could not eat or sleep, I was so excited about him. I felt as bad as if my brother had been in the same position.

The women knowing I felt sad, tried every way to aggravate me; some saying, "I know he is a murderer. I know he killed my brother, sister, or some other relative." I would reply, "If he had done such things, how could you be so friendly with him?" for these same women would come in and laugh, sing, and play cards with him very often, and women from the neighborhood of Forest City, used to comb his hair, arrange his neck-tie, and after he was arrested, abused him shamefully.

When Chaska was to be tried, I was called upon to testify. I told them all I could say would be in his favor; they thought it very strange I could speak in favor of an Indian. I went to court, and was put under oath. He was present, and I shook hands with him. I am particular in relating every interview I had with him, as many false and slanderous stories are in circulation about me.

He was convicted of being an accomplice in the murder of George Gleason, without any evidence against him. I was angry, for it seemed to me as if they considered my testimony of no account; for if they had believed what I said, he would have been acquitted. All the evidence was his own statement, wherein he said that he snapped his gun at Mr. Gleason; but through misinterpretation, it was made to appear as if he intended to try to kill him.

I know he had no more idea of killing the man than I had, or did no more towards it than I did. He was present, so was I; and they might as well hang me as him, for he was as innocent as myself.

After Mr. Gleason was dead, as we rode away from his body, I heard Chaska say to Hapa, "Get out and shoot him again; don't leave him with any life to suffer." Hapa said, "You have not shot to-day; you go with me, and I will go." They they both got out, giving me the lines to hold, and went to the body, but he was still motionless. Hapa fired at him; Chaska raised his gun, but it snapped fire. I don't believe his gun was loaded at all. That was what convicted him. Afterwards, in speaking to me of the affair, he said he had done as he would wish any one to do by him. He was afraid there was a little life, and he wished to put him out of his suffering.

I know that after he was convinced I said many things I need not have said, and would not at ordinary times; but every one ought to know that my mind was in a dreadful state, living as I had for six weeks in continual fear and anxiety, and I was not capable of acting rationally. The Indian who saved George Spear's life was lauded to the skies, and I could not refrain from saying that I considered my life and two children as valuable as his; but the Indians that saved me must be imprisoned, while that Indian was carried around and shown as a great hero.

I soon discovered that the Commission was not acting according to justice, but by favor; and I was terribly enraged against them. The more angry I got, the more I talked, making matters worse for Chaska as well as myself. I can now see wherein I failed to accomplish my object. They soon at the camp began to say, "I was in love," that "I was his wife," that "I preferred living with him to my husband," and all such horrid abominable reports. I know I am innocent; that I acted from right motives; and sure am I if I am condemned here on earth, God will see me righted, if not here, I hope in heaven.

I never could love a savage, although I could respect them; and I would willingly do all in my power to benefit the Indian tribe. I had strong feelings of gratitude towards all of them, with one exception; that is Hapa. I am very sorry, but do not, I beg of you, my readers, expect me to feel as you that have suffered at their hands. I do not know of but two females that were abused in that

Indian camp last summer. I often asked females, as we heard such reports; but they all said they were treated well that I saw.

I think it was two days before I left Camp Release that I went to the Indian camp. Miss E. B. – – accompanied me. I saw Chaska's mother, and such a cry burst forth from her at the sight of me! She put her arms around me, saying, "My boy! my boy! they will kill him! Why don't you save him? He saved your life, many times; you have forgotten the Indians, now your white friends have come." I was much affected at her reproaches, and I told her I was doing everything I could to save him, but that the Indians were lying about him. She told me she had been to carry him some bread, but the soldiers would not let her go in where he was, and she begged me to go and see him. I had not been before that day, although I had been asked many times to go. The women from our tent were going every day to see the Indian prisoners, but I had always refused to accompany them, telling them I had seen enough of the Indians for the present. I knew it would make me feel sad to see the poor wretches tied together like beasts.

This day, when I returned to camp, I went to the prisoners' tent, accompanied by Major Collin and Miss E. B – –. When I entered I went towards Chaska to shake hands, but he refused to take my hand.

I inquired what was the cause of his acting so unfriendly. He said I had told falsehoods to the soldiers, or I would not now see him tied hand and foot. He then repeated all he had done for me and my children, and reproached me for so forgetting his kindness. It affected me to tears, for he spoke of many things he had done, such as selling his coat for flour, sleeping without his blanket so my children might be warm, etc. I said to him that I had lost all my friends now by trying to save him, and it was very wrong for him to blame me. I am not ashamed to acknowledge I cried. I am naturally very sensitive, and cannot see tears or hear reproaches without shedding tears.

I at last convinced him that I was not to blame for his being in imprisonment, and I said I would like to shake hands and bid him goodbye in friendship. He shook hands with me, and that is all that passed between us. I never saw him again, for I left very soon for my home.

There were at that time twenty-one Indians all fastened together by their feet. I did not go any nearer to him than four feet. But there have been outrageous reports put in circulation of that visit I made to that poor forsaken creature. Any one doubting my story may inquire of the persons who were with me—not the soldiers. I was not aware of the excitement that existed throughout the country. I knew there had been awful murders committed, but I knew not the particulars, or how many people were enraged against the Indians. I was so happy, and rejoiced so greatly, over my safe deliverance from death and dishonor, through the kindness of the Indians, that I wished to sound their praises far and near.

That night, before leaving, I heard from Capt. Grant that Chaska would not be executed, but would be imprisoned for five years. I was very well contented, and troubled myself no farther; for he gave me his word as a gentleman that that was the truth.

He cautioned me not to speak of it, as it was a secret. I never told anyone until he was dead.

I came from Camp Release with four ladies who had been prisoners. We were sent without any escort over seventy miles, through the scene of those awful murders. The day before we left, Sibley sent down a train of forty wagons, and a number of prisoners, mostly French and German, with eighty soldiers as an escort. When we got to Yellow Medicine I found them there, on their way to Wood Lake to camp for the night, and we ladies proposed camping with them, as the man who drove our team said he was going to Redwood to camp, saying there was no danger, for there were no Indians within one hundred miles of us, except those at Camp Release. I got frightened, as usual, and said I was afraid to go on to Redwood to camp; for I had suffered so much in that neighborhood I cared not to stay there over night; so I concluded to leave the horse team, and stay with the ox train, as I saw a lady in the train that I knew very well. Mrs. H – – and I remained at the soldiers' camp until after supper, when we proposed to go back to Yellow Medicine—three miles—and stay in the tepees. The farmer Indians were then under Major Galbraith's directions, digging potatoes. We went to John Moore's tepee, and stayed with his family all night. Capt. McClarthy promised to wait for us; but when we arrived at the camp they had all gone; not a vestige of the camp was discernible.

I afterwards learned that the wagon master, hearing of our going to the tepees, said he would hurry on; and if I liked the tepees so well, I might stay there, for he was going to hurry off.

Capt. Kennedy and one of his soldiers were detailed to come for us in the morning from the camp of soldiers that were guarding the Indians, and they were only ordered to take us to Wood Lake. Now we were in great trouble; they dared not go any farther without orders, and we did not wish to stay at the tepees. The soldiers at length decided to go on with us to Fort Ridgely without orders, thinking we could overtake the other teams when they stopped for dinner at Redwood. Mrs. H – – and myself traveled in great fear all day. I was now going towards the spot where poor Gleason was killed, and she where her dead husband laid, still unburied. We imagined Indians in every bush. We had but one gun, and now I think how reckless we were to start on such a journey in such an unprotected way.

The men laughed at our fears, but I told them Mr. Gleason also laughed, going over the same road; and I felt sure there were Indians now near us, for Little Crow sent one hundred men the night before the battle of Wood Lake, and they had never returned to camp. No one can imagine my feelings as I passed poor Gleason's grave, for he was now covered from sight; the whole scene was again before my eyes. I got so nervous that my teeth chattered, and I shook like one with the palsy. As we got to the river, my fears increased, for it was a dreary place. Now we had to go down through the woods for some ways, and we all expected to be fired on by Indians hiding in the bushes; but God in his mercy delivered us from death by them, for it afterwards proved that Indians were secreted in those woods. We at last arrived at Little Crow's village; the buildings were all standing, and everything was looking well, only so desolate; not a sound to break the stillness, not a living thing visible. The soldiers proposed leaving the road and going to a farm house to get some corn for their horses, for we had all come without breakfast. We sat in the wagon, Mrs. H., myself and children, while they gave the horses feed; and while they were eating, the men roamed through the gardens, gathering tomatoes, &c. In a few minutes after they left we heard a dog bark, and I told Mrs. H. there were Indians in the neighborhood. In a moment we heard a gun, and then another; Mrs. H – – being much alarmed, jumped and ran into a corn field. As she did so I saw two Indians just going down into the woods, not ten rods from where we sat. I beckoned to the men, and they very hurriedly hitched up the horses, and they drove them on a run for the other teams which we had seen some three miles beyond us, on a hill. The soldiers' object in going that way was to save five miles, but we came near losing our lives by so doing. As we drove over the prairie, regardless of road or track, we turned, and five Indians were coming towards us on foot, running very fast. About that time, the teams on the hill seeing us, and think-ing we were Indians, started some men to capture us. The Indians, seeing the horsemen, turned around and made for the woods, where we could see their tepees. We were very glad to keep with the train; and we arrived at the Fort at five o'clock that evening, very tired, but, oh, how happy to be within its walls. How refresh-ing that bath, and the clean clothes, given us by the kind lady of the Surgeon, and with what feelings of joy I laid myself and the little ones down to rest, undressed—it being the first time I had taken my clothes off to sleep, in nearly eight weeks.

The next morning, as Mrs. H – – and I were preparing for breakfast, my little boy exclaimed, "There is my father!"—and so it was. There was my husband I had mourned as dead, now living—coming towards me. I was happy then, and felt that I would have died then willingly; and said "Thy will not mine be done," for I knew my children had a protector now.

I left the Fort about noon that day, and arrived at Shakopee in a few days. I did not hear any more respecting Chaska, but felt that it was all right with him. I was in Red Wing when the President sent on the list of those that were to be executed. I noticed the name of Chaskadon, but knew it was not his number, and knew he was not guilty of the crime that Chaskadon was to be punished for.

Sunday after the execution, when the papers were brought in, I noticed my name immediately, and I saw that a mistake had been made. The Indian who was named Chaskadon, that the President ordered to be hanged, killed a pregnant woman and cut out her child; and they hung Chaska who was only convicted of being present when Mr. Gleason was killed. After passing eight weeks in Red Wing, I returned to St. Paul. I then saw Rev. S.R. Riggs, formerly missionary among the Sioux, and who was present at the time Chaska was hung, and he said he was really hanged by mistake, as his name was on the list that were recommended to mercy.

In a letter I received, he explained the matter in this way:

Mrs. Wakefield:

Dear Madam: —"In regard to the mistake, by which Chaska was hung, instead of another, I doubt whether I can satisfactorily explain it. We all felt a solemn responsibility, and a fear that some mistake should occur. We had forgotten that any other (except Robert Hopkins, who lived by Dr. Williamson's) was so called. On that fatal morning we never thought of the third one. When the name Chaska was called, your protector answered by the name, and came out, &c.

Respectfully yours,

S.R. Riggs

Now, I never will believe that all in authority at Mankato had forgotten what Chaska was condemned for, and I am sure, in my own mind, it was done intentionally. I dare not say by whom, but there is one who knoweth every secret, either bad or good, and the time will come, when he will meet that murdered man, and then he will find the poor Indian's place is far better than his own.

If the President had not plainly stated what the man was convicted for, then, probably there might have been a mistake but as it was, it was either carelessness, or, as I have said before, intentional, for every man was numbered as he was arrested, and the President sent the number, as well as the cause of his punishment. It has caused me to feel very unkindly towards my own people, particularly those in command at Mankato. There has been all kinds of reports in circulation respecting Chaska and I, but I care not for them. I know I did what was right, that my feelings were only those of gratitude towards my preserver. I should have done the same for the blackest negro that Africa ever produced; I loved not the man, but his kindly acts.

There are many things I would like to speak about in this narrative, but I would be obliged to mention particular names, and I will forbear; but I will say this, that many persons told entirely different stories respecting their treatment, after Sibley came, than they did before. One lady very often visited me, and she often complained of being uncomfortable from eating so heartily, but said the squaws forced her to eat, as that is their way of showing kindness towards a person. How many times I have listened to her telling the soldiers that she was nearly starved by the squaws, going days without food of any kind. It shocked me, and I reprimanded her severely for telling such untruths; but she was only one of a class of females that were endeavoring to excite the sympathies of the soldiers. My object was to excite sympathy for the Indians, and in so doing, they lost all respect for me, and abused me shamefully; but I had rather have my own conscience than that of those persons that turned against their protectors, those that were so kind to them in that great time of peril.

All the time I was with the Indians the women seemed to be envious of me, saying that the Indians thought more of me than any other female. They did of course think more of me than they did of strangers, for they had known me many years.

I could talk with them of things that had transpired in Shakopee that they knew about, and they considered me an old friend. No Indian ever came to my house that was hungry, without being fed, or if in need of clothes, I gave if I possibly could do so; they all came to me for medicine as much as they did to my husband, both in Shakopee and Yellow Medicine, and their actions have proved the Bible true to me, for it says, "Cast your bread upon the waters, and after many days it shall return to you."